THE WAY OF ST. FRANCIS

T0017237

THE WAY OF ST. FRANCIS

*The Challenge of Franciscan Spirituality
for Everyone*

MURRAY BODO, o.f.m.

IMAGE BOOKS
A Division of Doubleday & Company, Inc.
Garden City, New York
1985

Image Books edition published March 1985 by
special arrangement with Doubleday & Company, Inc.

Library of Congress Cataloging in Publication Data

Bodo, Murray.
The way of St. Francis.

Includes bibliographical references.
1. Spiritual life—History of doctrines—Middle ages,
600-1500.   2. Francis, of Assisi, Saint, 1182-1226.
I. Title.
BX2350.2.B6   1984   271′.3
Library of Congress Catalog Card Number 83–14066
ISBN: 0-385-19913-9

ACKNOWLEDGMENTS

"Francis of Assisi: An Introduction" first appeared in altered form in *Our Sunday Visitor,* October 4, 1981, and is reprinted with permission of Our Sunday Visitor, Inc.

Portions of Chapter 2 ("Making Peace") and Chapter 3 ("Living the Gospel") first appeared in *St. Anthony Messenger,* October 1982, and are reprinted with permission.

"Canticle of Brother Sun" from *St. Francis of Assisi: Writing and Early Biographies: English Omnibus of the Sources for the Life of St. Francis,* edited by Marion Habig, is reprinted with kind permission of the Franciscan Herald Press.

Excerpts from *The Selected Poetry of Rainer Maria Rilke,* edited and translated by Stephen Mitchell, copyright © 1982 by Stephen Mitchell, reprinted with kind permission of Random House, Inc.

Excerpts from *The Fool of God: Jacopone da Todi* by George Peck, copyright © 1980 by George Terhune Peck, reprinted with kind permission of the University of Alabama Press.

"The Big Rock Candy Mountains," Collected, Adapted and Arranged by John A. Lomax and Alan Lomax TRO, copyright © 1947, renewed 1975, by Ludlow Music, Inc., New York, N.Y. Used by permission.

Excerpts from *Poems of Gerard Manley Hopkins,* edited by W. H. Gardner and N. H. MacKenzie, are reprinted with permission of Oxford University Press.

Excerpts from "Birches" from *The Poetry of Robert Frost,* edited by Edward Connery Lathem. Copyright 1916, © 1969 by Holt, Rinehart and Winston. Copyright 1944 by Robert Frost. Reprinted by permission of Holt, Rinehart and Winston, Publishers.

An altered version of the Afterword was previously published in *Catholic Update,* March 1979, St. Anthony Messenger Press.

To My Mother and Father

CONTENTS

PREFACE

When I first put on the habit of St. Francis, I was eighteen years old. A lot has changed since then, in me and in the world around me. The Francis I know today is not the Francis I knew at eighteen, but his values and the stories that are told about how he lived and what he said continue to motivate the way I choose to live.

Francis of Assisi gave me a way of life that keeps challenging me and troubling me and making me look again at the possibilities within and around me. I keep returning to Francis and his interpreters to find help in understanding my own experience.

From Francis and the early Franciscans I have learned that there are no rigid "ways" to God; there are only those who make their way to God and who leave us a record of their journey. The writings of St. Francis are such a document: They are personal, simple, and direct in a way that those of his great interpreters, such as St. Bonaventure, are not. Bonaventure is called the second founder of the Order of St. Francis, and he is the most important medieval commentator on Franciscan spirituality.

But there is a great difference in style between the poet Francis, and the scholar Bonaventure. One is intuitive, nonrational, caught up with concrete, specific things; the other is discursive, rational, concerned with abstract ideas and concepts, with truth. You have only to read the *Testament* of Francis and *The Soul's Journey into God* by the theologian Bonaventure to see how different are the styles of these two great saints. *The*

Soul's Journey into God maps out symbolically and systematically how *one would* ascend to God. The *Testament* of Francis records quite simply how Francis and the earthly brothers did in fact respond to God.

For both Francis and Bonaventure the *way* is the Gospel of Jesus Christ. But in Francis there is no logical system of living the Gospel as in Bonaventure, no hierarchic, overall structure like a cathedral. There is only the response to God's Word that restores crumbling chapels. Bonaventure's writings are like a great Gothic cathedral; Francis' writings are like the little chapel of the Portiuncula which he restored and which today is protected inside a huge Bonaventure-like basilica. Both of them are houses of God, but their ambience, their feel, is totally different. The house of God you build or restore depends on who you are. Both the basilica and the wayside chapel are houses of God; it is the builders who are different.

I'm not sure what kind of builder I am, if I build at all. I surely don't build cathedrals or even repair churches, nor like St. Bonaventure am I able to construct a magnificent, protective structure over the church Francis restored. I merely visit both and seem always to find there, or more often outside along the way, some little spot which I love and become enthused about, so that I want to polish it up and show it to others. There is nothing to conceal or cover over or protect in polishing; it allows what is there to shine through. This book contains some of my rubbings. Most of them I made on the way to or from the house of God.

FRANCIS OF ASSISI:
AN INTRODUCTION

His life reaches back eight centuries to the year 1182, to a small Italian town in the Umbrian Valley. He is born to the cloth merchant, Pietro Bernardone and his French wife, the Lady Pica. He is baptized Giovanni, which his father later changes to Francesco. His youth is spent in relative luxury, in gaiety and music, in the enviable role of leader among his peers. He is a young man of charm and wit, of kindness, good humor, and the prodigal generosity of a wealthy, spoiled son. And his consuming ambition is to be a knight after the fashion of his heroes, the legendary knights-errant of the court of King Arthur and the paladins of Charlemagne.

And so in his twentieth year he rides off to battle in a minor skirmish between Assisi and its neighboring city, Perugia. The citizens of Assisi are routed, and Francis is taken prisoner at Ponte San Giovanni, a small village between Assisi and Perugia. For a year he is in a Perugian prison cheering his fellow prisoners and in general making the best of a difficult situation, a pattern that will recur throughout his life.

Because of his wealth and position Francis is imprisoned with the nobles, not with the common citizens, a distinction and a separation that begins to haunt and trouble the young Francis. But even in the somewhat better quarters of the nobility, the damp, squalid conditions of the prison finally begin to work on his delicate constitution, and Pietro Bernardone is able to ransom his son on the grounds of illness.

When he is finally released and returned to his native Assisi,

Francis spends the year 1204 bedridden—another kind of imprisonment, another year of testing. And when he finally rises from his bed, he walks the hills of Assisi disconsolate, for the world has lost its splendor. A light has gone out inside him; he no longer sees with the bright eyes of a child. It is here in the desert of his desolation that he begins to hear the voices and see the visions that will transform his life, that will turn him into a child again.

The first voice comes in a dream in the city of Spoleto, where Francis is bivouacked in another futile attempt to break out of his doldrums by going off to war as a knight. He sees the large room of a castle whose walls are covered with shields, and a voice proclaims they belong to Francis and his followers. Misinterpreting the dream, Francis is ready to embrace this prophecy of knighthood and glory when he hears another voice:

"Francis, is it better to serve the Lord or the servant?"

"Oh, sir, the Lord, of course."

"Then why are you trying to turn your Lord into a servant?"

And like the prophet Samuel, Francis recognizes the voice that is speaking to him.

"Lord, what do you want me to do?"

"Return to Assisi. There it shall be revealed to you what you are to do, and you will come to understand the meaning of this vision."

And so it is that Francis begins to listen to God instead of his own impatient desire for glory on the battlefield. He starts the long, inner journey back to Assisi.

How great must be Francis' humiliation when he rides into Assisi alone. The supreme test of the knight is his courage; he would prefer death in battle to anything that would appear like a shrinking from the fight. And yet, in obedience to God's Word, Francis comes home a solitary knight who has left the battlefield. This courage of his convictions in the face of shame and humiliation becomes a hallmark of Francis' personality, so that to the end of his life he never wavers once he is convinced that some course of action is the will of God.

Of course, turning from the battlefield is not something Francis does easily and in one quick decision. It costs him great mental suffering. That whole year after returning from Spoleto Francis spends praying in a cave outside Assisi, trying to come to terms with God's will, allowing God to purify his heart. And somewhere in all that struggle, out of the visions and revisions of his dreams, Francis finds the philosophers' stone that transforms the base metal of his knightly ideals into something very fine and high and at the same time foolish and full of paradox: the knight comes down off his charger and becomes a fool and singer at court. Not just the usual fool for Christ but a court fool with all that implies of wisdom and influence in the lives of everyone in the miniworld of medieval society. He becomes a man who is listened to, a man whose foolishness is wiser than the wisdom of sages.

How does that happen? Like so much of the mystery of anyone's life, there is no single incident that constitutes his moment of transformation. Rather what happens to Francis is the result of several important events whose cumulative effect is to show him the deeper movement of his heart, the direction he has been heading all along, had he been aware of what was going on in his heart. The effect of his experiences is so powerful that he begins to hear within a voice more true than the voices around him, the voices of his own milieu and the values they represent.

And the voice within is the voice he hears one day while praying before the crucifix in the little run-down chapel of San Damiano: "Francis, go and repair my house which, as you see, is falling into ruins."

San Damiano is in fact falling into ruin, so Francis immediately sets off to repair the little church. He takes literally the Lord's words and because he does, he ends up repairing the bigger house of the Lord, the Church itself. He who is the son of the wealthiest Assisi merchant rushes home, snatches a bale of cloth from his father's shop, mounts his horse, and speeds off to the neighboring town of Foligno. There he sells the cloth and the horse and hikes back to the church of San Damiano. He offers the money to an astonished priest who recognizes Francis and refuses to accept the money because he rightfully suspects that this prodigality is taking place without the knowledge or approval of Francis' father. The disappointed Francis flings the money onto the windowsill and sets out for Assisi to beg stones to repair God's church.

Another turning point in Francis' life: you repair God's house not with money but with stones acquired by overcoming your shame and begging. And the stones people give to a beggar become the living Church.

No one can go around begging stones and dressing like a beggar without attracting attention; and when that someone is the richest young man in town, that attention naturally turns into ridicule and scorn. So one day as Francis is begging in Assisi's streets and the crowd is mocking him and catcalling after him, his father hears the noise and goes to the door of his shop to see what is happening. To his great dismay and shame he sees his own son being mocked through the streets. Pietro is enraged at this insult to the family honor. Only a few months before when Francis sold the cloth and the horse, Pietro had dragged him home and locked him up in a storage room. But when Pietro had to leave on a buying trip, Lady Pica braved her husband's wrath and released Francis, who went immediately to live with the poor priest of San Damiano. And now this! It is too much for Pietro; he rushes into the street and drags his son before the Bishop of Assisi, demanding that Francis return the money for the cloth and horse.

And this is how it was: Calmly Francis strips himself of his clothes in a ritual act reminiscent of the Baptism of the early Christians, and there before the crowd gathered in the bishop's courtyard, he lays his clothes at his father's feet and utters the most dramatic words of his life: "Listen to me, everybody! Until now, I have called Pietro Bernardone my father! But now that I am determined to serve God, I return not only his money, but all the clothes I have from him! From now on, I can walk naked before the Lord, no longer saying, 'my father, Pietro Bernardone,' but, 'our Father who art in Heaven!' "

In this dramatic episode of rejecting his father, Francis becomes a public person. He calls upon everyone present to witness what he is doing. He is publicly leaving his father for the Kingdom of God; and the rest of his life he conducts himself like one who expects people to hold him accountable for his actions.

The man of God, however, is still a knight at heart; he will wear his religious life with honor and integrity. His code will be the chivalry and sincerity of the Gospel, and he expects the world to hold him to his commitment. And thus begins one of the greatest spiritual odysseys in history: the journey of Francis from his father's house to the house of his heavenly Father. For Francis that father is the Father revealed by Jesus, and the journey to Him is the way that follows in the footsteps of Jesus Christ.

Francis immediately begins in earnest to live the Gospel literally and without compromise, and the authenticity of his life begins to attract others. The first of many to follow Francis' example is a wealthy merchant of Assisi named Bernard of Quintavalle. So taken is he with the change in Francis' life that he invites Francis to his home. After the evening meal the two men retire for the night, and Francis pretends to fall asleep immediately. Then Bernard also feigns sleep and begins to snore. At the sound of Bernard's snoring, Francis rises from bed and kneels on the floor repeating over and over all night long, "My God and my all." The astonished Bernard is deeply moved and in the morning asks Francis what he must do to become God's servant.

The response of Francis is a key to his whole manner of discerning God's will. He asks Bernard to accompany him to morning Mass at the church of St. Nicholas. After Mass, Francis asks the priest to open the book of the Gospel three times. And this is where the pages fall:

"If you wish to be perfect, go and sell all your possessions and give to the poor . . . and come, follow me."
"Take nothing for your journey, neither staff nor knapsack, shoes nor money."
"If any man will come after me, let him renounce self, take up his cross and follow me." (Mt. 19:21; Lk. 9:3; Mt. 16:24)

And that is what Bernard does, beginning a movement of men and women that will become the three Orders of St. Francis.

It is of no little significance that Francis asks the *priest* to open the Gospels. From the very beginning the Little Poor Man of

Assisi is a man of the Church, a fact that can easily be overlooked in romanticizing his personal journey to God. Francis is indeed radical, but he is radical within the Church. He consistently turns to the Church to discern what is taking place within him and his followers. He writes in his last testament, "The Lord gave me, and still gives me, so great a confidence in priests who live according to the law of the Holy Roman Church, that even if they sought to persecute me, I would nonetheless keep coming back to them."

So great is Francis' reverence for the priesthood that he considers himself unworthy of it and never accepts ordination for himself. He is an ordained deacon of the Church, but never a priest, and he intends his Order to be a nonclerical Order of brothers.

Most of the delightful stories of St. Francis come out of the early years of his brotherhood when he and his companions go about the countryside preaching and healing, working in the fields, and begging alms. The charm of these stories is that they are love stories, a curious combination of tales of courtly love and the Acts of the Apostles told by a court fool in the manner of parables or medieval allegories. Always there is chivalry and derring-do and courtesy acted out against the background of building the Kingdom by the foolishness of the Cross.

Story after story in early Franciscan lore deals with the affective powers of the soul and their purification. Stories like Francis overcoming his own squeamishness and pettiness in embracing lepers; Francis coming to grips with his own darker side, his violent shadow self, when he tames the wolf of Gubbio, an allegorical story of the individual confronting the violence of his own heart by embracing his potential for violence and letting the Lord redeem what he is courageous enough to look at.

The final seal and approval of the way of St. Francis is a dramatic event which takes place on a lonely mountain about a hundred miles north of Assisi, two years before he dies. The mountain is called La Verna, and Francis retires there in early September 1224 in order to prepare for the Feast of St. Michael the Archangel. The prayer of Francis on La Verna is the key to who he is and why he has had such an impact on history: "O

Lord, I beg of you two graces before I die—to experience personally and in all possible fullness the pains of your bitter Passion, and to feel for You the same love that moved You to sacrifice Yourself for us."

Only a lover can understand words like these, and only a man with a chivalrous heart can utter them. On La Verna, Francis the knight and Francis the lover merge in this final "foolish" request. Only the humility and genuineness of Francis' life save this prayer from a certain Quixote-like bravado. His whole life attests that this prayer is made unselfconsciously from the heart, his eyes fixed on Jesus, with no glance to the side to see if anyone is watching. Like the prayer which Bernard of Quintavalle hears Francis utter the whole night long, "My God and my all," Francis' request on La Verna is a lover's plea for total union with the beloved. And the beloved's "yes" is an embrace so complete that Francis' side and hands and feet are sealed with the wounds of love, the marks of the Passion of Christ on his flesh. In a very real sense Francis becomes a further enfleshment of the living God. It is almost as if his adopted Father, not satisfied with adoption, has made Francis His son physically, sealing him with the brand marks of his only begotten Son, Jesus Christ.

Francis lives two more years after receiving the stigmata at La Verna, a protracted Calvary of the body and soul. When he leaves the mystic mountain, the trachoma he has had for years worsens, and he asks to be taken to San Damiano, where, in a small hut next to the convent of St. Clare, he spends over fifty days in physical and spiritual darkness. During those days and nights, Jesus embraces Francis' soul as he had his body on La Verna, and Francis experiences what Jesus felt when he cried out on the cross, "My God, my God, why have you forsaken me?"

Francis feels abandoned by his Divine Lover, whose embrace he had felt so totally on Mount La Verna. Had their love been consummated only to be frustrated henceforth like the love of the knight and the lady in the code of courtly love? In the darkness, with his own doubts and the wounding of God as his only companions, Francis hears a voice out of the silence:

"Francis, if in exchange for all these evils, you were to receive a treasure so great that the whole earth, changed into gold, would be nothing beside it, would you not have reason to be satisfied?"

"Certainly, Lord."

"Then, be happy, for I guarantee you that one day you shall indeed enjoy the Kingdom of Heaven, and this is as certain as if you possessed it already."

And the stone rolls back from Francis' heart, and he rises from the cave of self forever. The treasure he sought in the cave as a young man is finally his. And in his ecstasy Francis sings the great poem of his life, a canticle of gratitude to the Father, *The Canticle of Brother Sun.*

In this canticle Francis unconsciously and unselfconsciously reveals the depths of his soul, where a profound reconciliation of opposites has taken place. He takes the four medieval elements of earth, water, air, and fire and unites them in binary sexual combinations. They become brother and sister, a symbolic union of the male and female dimensions of his soul that have come together in a wholeness of integration. And the cosmic dimension of the poem becomes an unconscious mirror of his own soul, thus reconciling the cosmic and psychic dimensions of reality. *The Canticle of Brother Sun* thus becomes one of the great poems of reconciliation, effecting in a few simple strokes what the great poets of the world have spent a lifetime doing: integrating outer and inner experience in an art object which exists apart from them, fine and beautiful and true.

In his final two years after receiving the stigmata, Francis continues to preach and witness as a herald of the Great King. And when he dies on October 3, 1226, a light is seen over Mount Subasio, a light that is still there on the mountain, filtering down its slopes into Assisi where you sense it, feel it in your bones. And the words of Francis on his deathbed ring in your soul: "I have done what is mine to do; may Christ teach you what is yours to do."

1

Poverty

If you were to ask anyone what comes immediately to mind at the mention of the name "St. Francis," most people would say "poverty." He is "Il Poverello," the Little *Poor* Man of Assisi; and it is precisely his poverty which has been most hotly debated and most misunderstood.

In the midst of all the smoke and fire over the issue of poverty stands the simple Francis. For him poverty was never an end in itself, but a means to the indwelling of God and a way of life that makes present the Kingdom of God. In what is probably the earliest "biography" of St. Francis, a little allegorical work entitled *Sacrum Commercium (The Holy Exchange Between Francis and Lady Poverty),* the core of Francis' relationship to poverty is sketched in a few deft lines. The first reason for his love of poverty is that *holy poverty stands high above all the virtues that prepare in us a dwelling place for God, and it is right that it stands first both in place and in name among all the other Gospel virtues.*

And the second reason for the pre-eminence of poverty in Francis' way to God is that *the Son of God loved this virtue especially; he went in search for it and found it, when he effected our salvation upon earth. And when he began to preach, he entrusted holy poverty as a light into the hands of those who enter the door of faith, and he set it as the cornerstone of his house.*

Then in two sentences that speak volumes, the author of this early portrait says neatly, *The other virtues only promise the*

Kingdom of Heaven, but poverty makes the Kingdom present here and now. "Blessed are the poor in spirit," Jesus said, "for theirs is the Kingdom of Heaven."

Francis and the early brothers took literally to heart the words of Jesus, made them their own by living them, and expected what the words promised to be effected in their lives. And so it happened. For to the citizens of Assisi and the surrounding towns where the brothers preached and witnessed, it seemed in fact that the brothers' lives did make present the Kingdom of God.

How different is the thinking of Francis from those of us who fret about what is to be *done* to build up the Kingdom of God, as if *we* are the ones to bring about God's Kingdom on earth. For Francis it is sufficient to be poor out of love for the Poor Christ. The Kingdom is made present when God takes up his dwelling among us; and, as Francis reads the Gospel, God takes up his dwelling only when we are poor in spirit. It is not what we do that brings about the Kingdom, but what we embrace that God might dwell among us.

What then are the implications of living out the first of the beatitudes? *The Legend of the Three Companions,* a fourteenth-century Franciscan work, tells how Francis became poor in spirit. As a young man, he, like any young man, wanted to do something with his life, become someone, make a contribution that would be uniquely his. He was constantly asking God to enlighten his mind and heart.

Then, according to this *Legend, one day while Francis was praying fervently to God, he received his answer. "Oh, Francis, if you want to know my will, you will have to hate and detest everything which till this moment you have loved and longed to make your own. And once you begin to do this, everything that previously seemed sweet and pleasant to you will become bitter and unbearable; and the things you once shuddered over will bring you great sweetness and you will be at peace."*

These words contain the central motivating force in Francis' life of poverty. And whether Francis actually hears these words of God, or whether God speaks to his heart, or whether he is simply divinely inspired to grasp the gospel paradox that to lose one's life is to gain it, the point is that Francis acts in response to God's words.

His poverty is a way of acting, of choosing, rather than a passive victimhood that lets things happen to him. It is love and not, as is sometimes thought, self-hatred or the desire to punish himself for his sins that impels him to embrace Lady Poverty.

Shortly after this profound prayer experience, *as he is riding near Assisi, he meets a leper and is filled with an overpowering horror as he always is when he meets one of these sufferers; but this time he makes a great effort and overcomes his aversion. He dismounts, and kissing his hand, gives the leper a coin. The leper, somehow understanding, gives him the kiss of peace. Then Francis remounts his horse and rides away. From that day on he mortifies himself increasingly until, through God's grace, he wins a complete victory.*

A complete victory over what? It is clear from the answer to Francis' prayer and from this story which follows it that the victory is over the darkness and ignorance which does not see aright; it is a victory over blindness which sees lepers as repulsive, over ignorance which does not know that the poverty which presently makes me shudder will ultimately bring me the greatest sweetness and content, if I but kiss its hand.

Kissing the leper is the great moment of enlightenment for Francis, because it proves the truth of God's words to him. The poverty and deprivation Francis chooses to suffer for the rest of his life is really a kissing of the leper's hand, a further putting on of the mind of Christ that enables Francis to become poor, to see the world as God sees it.

2

Making Peace

St. Francis lives in a time in some ways not much different from
our own. People then, as now, believe they are living in apoca-
lyptic times, that the end of the world is near. There is war and
there are rumors of war. Pope and emperor are fighting for
control of Italian city-states, cities are armed camps facing one
another, the middle class is struggling to wrest power and control from the nobility. And Francis is very much a part of these
wars. Three times he goes off to battle as a knight. Already in his
twentieth year he fights in the war between Assisi and Perugia
and spends a year in prison. There he embraces another kind of
leper, a young nobleman who has been excluded by the other
prisoners because of his constant bickering and complaining.

By his cheerfulness and patience Francis is able to bring this
person out from behind those walls of his own making. And this
becomes a bold pattern in Francis' life: By love he helps people
to find the opening through their walls; then the gates of the
cities begin to open. The lepers, even symbolically, always live
outside the walls, and you have to pass through armed gates to
embrace them. That is Francis' formula for peace: You have to
come out from behind your defenses and risk embracing what is
seemingly repulsive and dangerous. Only then will there be
peace, and only love can make it happen. For Francis peace is
inseparable from peace of soul, and neither can be achieved
without the risk of loving your supposed or real enemies.

It is impossible to speak of peace without reverence, which is
a precondition for any true love. And it is his reverence which

makes St. Francis the supreme peacemaker, especially his reverence for words. In his book, *The Last Christian,* Adolf Holl writes that

> Francis picked up every piece of paper with writing on it that he found in the street or elsewhere in the dirt, to put it in a more becoming place—worried that it might have the name of Christ on it. Francis also never allowed . . . so much as a letter or syllable to be crossed out in the notes and messages he dictated. . . . Written characters had for Francis an altogether sacramental—no other word will do —quality, because they could be formed into the name of God. Francis' attitude of tender, nurturing care has a great deal to do with culture, in the original sense of the word.

How little reverence for words there is today in the propagandistic interchange among the leaders of the world and in the media which interpret their words for us. How can there be peace in the world when people no longer mean what they say or say what they mean? How can false letters be formed into the name of God, or for that matter, into any true name? And how can there be peace when words no longer derive from the Word?

When we no longer reverence words, we no longer reverence what they name. And ultimately we no longer know the name of anything. Unlike Adam, we walk in the garden and cannot give names to the things of our experience. The garden becomes a nightmare of threatening objects we cannot define, and we load our silos with missiles to defend ourselves from our own loss of humanity.

3

Living the Gospel

Francis' conversion and early years in the Lord are years living among and ministering to the lepers who live outside the walls of Assisi, and the rest of his life he spends drawing people out from behind the comfortable walls of their boredom and leading them down into the plain to form a new city, a new world where the rejected and despised are embraced and included and where there are no walls to keep anyone out or in.

And those on the plain will have no possessions, because for Francis violence and the will to exclude others and harm them is intimately tied to possessiveness. He tells his brothers that if they have possessions, then they will need arms to defend them. With staggering simplicity Francis leaps into the twentieth century, where the defending of possessions has reached its final madness in a nuclear arsenal that can only destroy everything it is supposed to defend. Francis understands that it is not war that needs to be outlawed, but the love of money, the greed of the human heart that is at the root of war and that brings us to such peril.

It cannot be anything other than wealth that wars defend, for *people* are destroyed by wars, while wealth flourishes with the production of more and more instruments for the destruction of people.

Francis' antidote to war is poverty, which frees him and his followers to embrace and include and give. They have no need to be defensive because they have nothing to defend. So strong is Francis' conviction that money is one of the sources of violence and hatred that he forbids his brothers even to handle money except to provide for the sick.

He says in his first Rule, *We should not have any more use or regard for money in any of its forms than for dirt.* Such a statement is surely extreme, and over the years since Francis' death the Church has tempered this extreme view in her periodic interpretations of his Rule. However, as we approach the twenty-first century and look around us at the extreme peril to which the love of money has brought us and how little charity there is among nations because of possessiveness and greed, then the position of Francis is not so extreme as it looks on paper. His is an extreme foolishness which is much more desirable than the extreme madness which our spiritual moderation has achieved. An extreme greed can only be countered by an extreme love, not by a watered-down mediocrity. And Francis of Assisi understands that. There can be no love in a world of hatred unless lovers are willing to go to counterextremes.

And this conviction is confirmed for Francis at the beginning of his conversion when he asks the priest to open three times and read for him from the book of the Gospels. The words are clear and uncompromising: *If you wish to be perfect, go and sell all your possessions, and give to the poor . . . and come, follow me.* (Mt. 19:21) *Take nothing for your journey, neither staff nor knapsack, shoes nor money.* (Lk. 9:3) *If any man will come after me, let him renounce self, take up his cross and follow me.* (Mt. 16:24)

Volumes have been written on how Francis of Assisi lives out these three texts. But here it is sufficient to say that Francis' poverty is not the brainchild of a radical social reformer. It is simply the response of a sincere man to the words of Jesus Christ. The radicalness of St. Francis is not in his poverty but in his response to the Gospel of Jesus. He *lives* it.

And that is what is so astounding to the people of his time. They don't think it can be done. Nor do we today. The life of Francis says that the Gospel is a way of life and not a series of platitudes to make us feel good on Sunday morning. Francis' whole life is a proclamation that the love of neighbor can only be secured when the Gospel is lived sincerely, when the Word of God moves people to make decisions that radically change their lives.

4

Francis and Money

The call of Francis, coming as it did at the beginning of the rise of Italian city-states and the emergence of a moneyed middle class, was a divine antidote to the disease which would infect society and, more importantly, the individual, from then on. One's personal value and self-esteem would by and large be measured in proportion to an ability to make money. Much of life, if you were to feel good about yourself, would be taken up with the acquisition of money. Money and what it represents becomes the fullness of life.

I do not think that Francis was a social reformer who saw what money would do to the fabric of society. He was rather the quintessential Christian who saw what money would do to the spirit. Christ alone is the fullness of life, and the compulsive pursuit of money, more than anything else, distracts the individual from what really brings life. And it is what happens at the core of the individual which ultimately determines what society will become.

For Francis all of life's energies are to be directed to laying up treasures in heaven rather than here where rust and moth consume. His stance, of course, is madness to most of us, who see such a viewpoint as a pipe dream, a naïve view of reality. And the history of the Franciscan Order has proven that the original vision of Francis was indeed unlivable except for a brief time at the beginning when he was still alive and the number of his followers was small. It would be a gross distortion of the truth to say that the Franciscan Order exists in the world without money; but the followers of Francis, even today, try not to measure their worth by how much money they receive for serving others—though the temptation to do so is always there.

The measure of the Franciscan way is still the fullness of life, and the measure of life is joy. True joy derives from seeking first the Kingdom of God, and it is that priority which infuses Francis' way with Spirit and Life. Francis spells out his way succinctly and simply in the first few words of the *Rule of 1223:* "In the name of the Lord! The Rule and life of the Lesser Brothers is this: to observe the Gospel of our Lord Jesus Christ by living in obedience, without property, and in chastity."

5

Repairing God's House

Francis used to say this prayer over and over again, hoping for some tangible response from God: *Most High, glorious God. Illumine the darkness of my heart. Give me a right faith, a certain hope and a perfect charity; and grant me insight and wisdom, so I can always observe your holy and true command.*

These are the first words we have of St. Francis, probably dating from 1205–6 when he was twenty-three years old. Fittingly, they are a prayer to the "Most High," a term he will continue to use for the rest of his life. That his first words are a prayer sets the tone and direction for everything that will follow, for always his first concern will be for the *spirit of prayer, and devotion,* and he will condemn any human activity that extinguishes them.

The word "devotion" in the writings of Francis does not indicate the pious attitude or demeanor with which it is so often associated today. Rather it means an eagerness and cheerfulness in doing the will of God. As soon as Francis hears the Word of God, he cannot rest until he puts it into practice. The light to the darkness of his heart; the faith, hope, charity; the insight and wisdom that he prays for are "so I can always observe your holy and true command."

His prayer is for the Most High to take the initiative with him, and it begins in the chivalrous, courteous address of praise: "Most High, glorious God." The prayer of Francis always begins and ends in praise. His is the prayer of adoration which recognizes the infinite distance between Creator and creature, which acknowledges his nothingness before the Most High God.

This nothingness or littleness is a theological statement and not, as we moderns sometimes think, a psychological one. Francis is not looking down upon himself or demeaning himself or looking at himself at all. He is looking at God and simply stating what for him is a fact: God is God and Francis is not a god. This perspective will color everything he is to become and everything he will do.

It was most probably while he was praying the above prayer, or something like it, that another turning point occurred in Francis' life. He was praying before the image of Christ crucified in the chapel of San Damiano when *a tender and compassionate voice spoke to him: "Francis, can't you see my house falling into ruin? Go, and repair it for me." Trembling with awe, Francis replied, "With joy will I do it, Lord."*

From then on his heart was smitten and wounded with love and compassion for the suffering Christ; and for the rest of his life he bore in his heart the wounds of the Lord Jesus. These words are the stuff of chivalry and romance, a kind of Grail legend in reverse. Instead of the young paladin sallying forth in search of the Grail, the Holy Grail comes to him, and he must spend the rest of his life in response to the gift of God.

That it is Christ *crucified* who speaks to Francis could easily be explained away as a projection of Francis' own conscience expressing its guilt and need to atone for his father's greed and violence, which he knows is inside himself as well. It *could* be explained that way, and for some it is the only explanation, because either they stop with Francis himself and refuse to hear the rest of the story, or they refuse to believe that God speaks through and from the depths of the self.

When the Grail does in fact come to someone, when God is truly speaking, it is not just the self speaking to itself, and it is never for one person alone; it is for all people. And so it is in this revelation to Francis in the little chapel of San Damiano. The house that Francis is to repair is not just this crumbling chapel, as Francis in his simplicity at first believes, but it is the larger house of God, as well, the Church itself. And the most important revelation to Francis, the "epiphany" that does restore the house of God, is that God is human. It is the human, suffering Christ who speaks to Francis, and it is that Christ whom Francis and the first brothers reveal and restore to the Church.

At the time of Francis' vision God had retreated from people into the golden eternity of Byzantine mosaics: stern, stylized, remote. And now through Francis, God is again incarnate. Francis prays with the psalmist, *Seek the Lord and his strength, seek always the face of the Lord.* And the face that is shown him is the *living* God's. He is warm and vulnerable. He is the baby Jesus who appears to Francis at Christmas Mass in the mountain hermitage of Greccio; He is the Byzantine crucifix whose lips soften and begin to speak *human* words; He is the lover who penetrates Francis' flesh with his own wounds. He is the human Savior who evokes a human response from Francis, who in turn answers the suffering, flesh-and-blood God with the wounds in his own flesh, the physical mortification that is part of his identification with his Lord. Like an apprenticed knight, a squire, Francis strives to follow in the footsteps of his Master.

And this response changes the whole heart and countenance of religion, as is reflected in the art which follows upon the Franciscan movement. No longer is God the stern Christ of the icon. Now he is limned in flesh colors drawn from human models, and the Renaissance is possible. The way Francis restores God's house is to remind people that God is human as well as divine; and he does this by living in total response to the words of the *Incarnate* God.

Thus the love story of Francis of Assisi begins, the story whose living out will bring God to earth again. And this is how it was: Before the Bishop of Assisi he publicly exchanges his earthly father for his heavenly Father by returning all his possessions to Pietro Bernardone and proclaiming before the assembled citizens of Assisi, . . . *from now on I will say, "Our Father who art in heaven," and not "my father Pietro Bernardone."* Then, the story continues, *he starts back to San Damiano gay and fervent, clothed like a hermit. But before he gets there, he turns back to the city, where he begins praising God loudly in the streets and piazzas; and when he finishes his song of praise, he starts beg-*

ging for stones to use in restoring the church. He calls to passersby, "Give me one stone and you will have one reward; two stones, two rewards; three stones, a threefold reward." He speaks from the heart, for he has been chosen by God to be simple and unlearned, using none of the erudite words of human wisdom; and in all things he bears himself with simplicity. Many people mock him as mad, but others are moved to tears.

Such was the response of Francis of Assisi, a man who lived in another age, another time.

If our following of St. Francis is basically medieval at heart, then we have failed to do in our lives what Francis did in his. St. Francis was a postconciliar man, putting into practice and implementing the decrees of Lateran Council IV, one of the great reform councils of the Church. He made the Gospel ring true for his own times, which is basically what any renewal in the Church is all about. The Gospel of Jesus Christ is eternal, and when it is no longer applicable, then the fault is in us who have not made the painful journey into ourselves and into our times to rediscover God's present Incarnation.

To try to imitate Francis rather than listen to the Lord in our own time as he did in his only stops time and absolves us from restoring God's house, which is once again falling into ruin.

What are the stones that will restore it, and who is the one who will listen and not be ashamed to beg, and what is the house of God? When we try to answer these questions by looking around us and within us rather than looking only to the past, we begin to live in our own time and place, and we begin to hear God's voice here and now. It is clear and unmistakable; it is the Word enfleshed in our world.

6

Learning to Pray

I

The prayer of Francis flows out of what he has been willing to embrace. He believes and tells his brothers that the reason we don't become saints is not that we cannot overcome sin, but that we are unwilling to overcome shame. And overcoming shame implies a willingness to embrace that which we mistakenly believe is unworthy or unclean or insignificant, whether it be in ourselves or in others.

There are two dramatic incidents in Francis' life which illustrate how he overcomes shame and how his prayer is made authentic through them. The first takes place at the very beginning of his conversion. He is living with a poor priest at the chapel of San Damiano. His father and mother do not know where he is, so *his father goes round the city inquiring about his son. When he learns where Francis is, he calls together his friends and neighbors and goes down to San Damiano.*

Francis is still new in the service of Christ; so when he hears about his pursuers and knows they are coming, he hides from his father's anger by creeping into a secret cave which he has prepared as a hiding place. There he stays for a whole month. He eats food brought to him secretly and prays continually with tears that the Lord deliver him from persecution and grant him the fulfillment of his desire to serve Him alone.

He fasts and prays unceasingly, not trusting in his own strength but relying wholly on God; and God fills his soul with

*unspeakable joy and a wonderful light until, glowing with an
inner radiance, he leaves the cave, ready to face his persecutors.
Light of heart, he climbs the road to Assisi.*

*When his friends and relatives spy him, they smother him
with insults, calling him a fool and a madman, and they hurl
stones and mud at him.*

*But Francis, who has become God's servant, pays them no
heed. Indifferent to their insults, he thanks God for everything.*

This story is an archetypal story in Francis' spirituality. It
contains the very roots and movement of his life in God. Initially, Francis hides from his father's anger by *creeping* into a
secret cave which he has prepared as a refuge. Like all of us at
the beginning of the emergence of the true self, he fears his
father's anger, he draws inward and hides, and he prays for the
wrong thing because he does not as yet have the courage to
become himself. He prays that the Lord will *deliver him from
persecution and grant him the fulfillment of his desire.* He does
not know as yet that the fulfillment of his desire involves persecution.

But because he perseveres, the Lord fills his soul with light,
and he leaves the cave where he is hiding and faces the insults
and blows of his persecutors. In overcoming his shame, he discovers his true self and is unmoved by persecution. And he
thanks God for *everything,* not just for what is pleasant, such as
his misguided desire to be delivered from persecution. In acting, in facing the consequences of his commitment to Christ,
Francis learns to pray correctly. Again and again in his life
Francis continues to overcome shame in order to know the
Lord and himself that he might pray with a pure heart.

Another incident takes place before his conversion on a pil-
grimage to Rome to the tomb of the Apostle Peter.

*On the steps at the entrance some beggars are asking for
money from those who come and go. Francis quietly borrows the
clothes of one of the beggars, exchanging them for his own.
Then, dressed in rags, he stands on the steps with the others,
begging for alms.*

*At the end of the day he changes back into his own clothes
and returns to Assisi, asking Jesus to show him the right way.*

Once again an act of overcoming shame precedes his prayer. He identifies with the outcasts of society; he sees the world through their eyes; he discovers his own dependence and littleness. And, the story concludes, *when he returns home, he doesn't tell anyone his secret, but turns to God who alone is his never-failing guide.*

This last statement is important in understanding the prayer life of Francis. He reverences and stands guard over that profound center where we stand face to face with God, that secret, sacred space where we commune intimately with God.

In spite of lip service to personal freedom in our day, there can occur in the name of freedom a surrender of freedom, a subtle subjection to the group, a conformity to "community" which is antithetical to authentic freedom. And once again it is Francis who strikes the balance for that precious autonomy that lies at the heart of true community.

He and his brothers are bound to one another with the strongest ties of brotherhood and love. But always each brother's treasure, which he has received from the Lord, is reverenced and fostered even to the point where one or several brothers stand guard over a brother's prayer so that he can neither be disturbed nor heard.

Francis himself writes a *Rule for Hermitages* that fosters that essentially contemplative spirit which is at the heart of the Franciscan charism.

And his own example at La Verna, shortly before he receives the stigmata, dramatizes Francis' wisdom regarding the sacredness of his own personal relationship with the Lord, an area that is sometimes rudely and forcibly invaded today under the pretext of "sharing," "group spiritual direction," or "the fostering of togetherness." Communion is not fostered by an invasion of that secret cavern within where we sit naked and vulnerable in the presence of God.

Of Francis at La Verna there is a charming, delicate story.

He is looking for a suitable place to spend in deeper solitude the Lent of St. Michael the Archangel, which begins on the feast of the Assumption of Our Lady. So he calls Brother Leo and says to him, "Go and stand in the door of the oratory of the brothers' hermitage, and when I call you, come to me."

Brother Leo goes and stands in the doorway, and St. Francis walks some distance away and calls loudly. And Leo, hearing Francis calling, hurries to him. But Francis says to him: "Son, let's look for a place more removed, from which you cannot hear me when I call you."

Then Francis sends for the other brothers and tells them that he intends to spend the Lent of St. Michael in that solitary place, where he can pray alone, away from the others. And so he asks them to build a poor hut for him there, where they cannot hear him if he shouts.

And when the hut is made, St. Francis says to them: "Go back now and leave me here alone, because with God's help I intend to spend Lent here without distraction. None of you is to come to me, and don't let anyone else come to me!"

We need to retire into solitude from time to time and say to others, especially those closest to us, "Go back and leave me here alone." And we need to know that when we return, we will not have to give an account of what the Lord has spoken in silence.

It is true that the early friars publicly acknowledge their faults and confess their sins to one another. But that happens only in an atmosphere where the precious treasure of each brother's individuality is reverenced and where special gifts of the Lord are kept secret or minimized with that exquisite good taste which characterizes everything Francis does.

It is one thing to acknowledge your faults and sins against your brothers or sisters; it is another thing to reveal to another who you really are. What special relationship is necessary, what trust must be there, what love proven over the years before you tell someone who you are! And even then there is risk involved and there must be some pressing reason or some deep moment of meeting that allows for the mystery of self-revelation. Otherwise, revelation cheapens into exposure, and prayer becomes impossible because of the disintegration of that center where you find your identity in God. By the hasty, irreverent exposure of the naked self, you scatter pearls of great price to those who cannot, should not, receive them. St. Francis never shares with others the voice he uses in prayer. He draws up his hood to cover his ecstasy; he prays to God in secret.

II

A poet is a poet whether he makes poems or not, but a writer is a writer only if he writes. Francis is a poet, but he does not spend his life making poems. He lives his life preaching and teaching and being poor instead; but because he is a poet, everything he does is infused with poetry. And when he prays, he prays like a poet.

Francis' first biographer, Thomas of Celano, says many things about Francis' prayer which, taken together, form a composite picture of a poet at prayer. Using Celano's description of how Francis prayed, I have drawn up a sort of canon of Franciscan prayer:

Make all of your time a holy leisure in which to inscribe wisdom in your heart.

When visitors or any other business disturbs you, it is better to interrupt your prayers than to end them. Then, afterwards, you can return to them again in your deepest center.

Retreat to places of solitude where not only your soul, but also your body, can relax with God.

When you experience the presence of the Lord, do not disclose this hidden manna, lest others become aware of the Bridegroom's touch.

Direct your attention and affection with your whole being to the one thing you are asking of the Lord, so that you are not so much praying as becoming yourself a prayer.

Do not neglect any visitation of the Spirit. Even when some business is pressing or you are on a journey, take time to respond to the touches of grace; taste the sweet manna in frequent snatches.

When you go on a journey, always stop to pray, remembering the story of Francis returning from Rome in the rain and how he dismounted his horse and stood for a long time in the drenching rain. For he used to say, "If the body tranquilly takes its food, which together with the body will become the food of worms, how peacefully and tranquilly should not the soul take its food, which is God himself."

Keep this story before you: One Lent Francis made a small vase, using only his spare time, so that he would not be completely absorbed with it. Then one day, while he was praying, he turned to look at the vase, and he felt that his interior self had been distracted from its fervor. And, sad that his heart's voice had been interrupted in its speaking to the ears of God, he said in front of the brothers: "Alas, what a worthless work that has such power over me that it can twist my mind to itself! I will sacrifice it to the Lord, whose sacrifice it has impeded." When he had said these words, he took the little vase and tossed it into the fire.

Francis' whole life of prayer is an intense energy that is simultaneously a letting go. He does not so much pray as, in the words of his first biographer, he becomes a prayer. Of all descriptions of Francis' prayer, this, I think, is the most revealing. It is a description that haunts me, because I know that the destiny of every person is somehow to become a living prayer. What that means is a highly individualized story, the story of how each person takes the soil of his or her fashioning and with hard toil becomes a sensitive instrument for listening to God's voice inside.

There is a profoundly moving statue of St. Francis at the mountain hermitage of La Verna that, from the first time I saw it on a cold, rain-driven afternoon, revealed to me the Francis of my own imagining. The statue resembles a rough, unfinished piece of clay into which some frenzied artist has gouged out eyes and ears and mouth, has rough-wrung arms and legs and twisted neck, and squashed the whole piece to the ground. But the sculpture itself is not passive clay; it is filled with energy, as if in receiving the rough blows and jabs of the sculptor, it has realized its destiny and is rising from the ground to seize the sculptor's hand in ecstasy. It is not only worked upon from without, it is pushing from some source within. This sculpture is always before me and rises in my dreams from some primordial clay within that unites me to all of humanity. It is the clay itself that becomes the prayer it is trying to realize in the mind and heart alone.

When our whole being becomes what we strive in spirit to achieve, then we have found that letting go which allows the heavy hand of God to fashion us into the twisted torso of Christ upon the cross. Only then do we cease praying and become a living prayer. How that happens is sketched briefly in the above canon. The shape of the prayer is as individual as the person who emerges, a living prayer.

III

I have been trying, since my thirteenth year, to pray. Sometimes it has gone well, sometimes not. But always my ability or nonability to pray has been directly related to my everyday life and to my knowledge of myself. When I begin to experience difficulty in prayer, it is usually because I am refusing to let go of my present understanding of who I am and preventing a new understanding from emerging.

For example, if I have clung to some ideal picture of who I should be and have denied another part of myself that is struggling to be born, then I am inauthentic; and the God I have been praying to is no longer real, because he was fashioned from that idealizing part of me that is now dying. As my former self dies, so does the inadequate god who is fashioned out of the need to have a divinity who conforms to whom the self thinks it should be.

However, when I let go and let myself grow and emerge by embracing all sides of myself, God is again accessible, because the true God is he who loves and affirms and redeems who I really am and not just who I would like to be. In other words, the acceptance of the truth about myself opens the way to the truth about God, and both truths are one at the prayerful center of the person.

True prayer demands honesty with myself, for it is only the real "I" who can talk with God. And I do not mean to imply here that only the integrated self can pray, but simply that honesty with myself enables me to pray correctly. If, for example, I need to be "worthy" or "perfect" or "holy" before I can pray, then I will probably not pray at all, or if I do, it will be a pseudo, self-satisfied self talking to itself rather than with God. We commune with God as we honestly are and not as we would like to be.

The idealized self is always dying in prayer, because it cannot bear the truth. And if we let it die and pray from who we are becoming, then our image of God changes as we understand more clearly who we are.

And our prayer changes accordingly. It may move from the adoration of the all-good God to bitter complaining and bickering with an unjust God who is letting me suffer or who is abandoning me for some reason. If I experience God as betraying me but say instead how wonderful and good he is, then I am praying a lie. God will only be who he is objectively if, while trying and wanting to believe that, I pray to him as I am experiencing him subjectively, for the good God redeems and corrects my honestly expressed but false understanding of who he is.

I believe this sincere wrestling with God is what Francis experienced during that torturous year in the cave at the beginning of his conversion and at other times throughout his life, culminating in the fifty days of darkness that preceded his singing of *The Canticle of Brother Sun.* He felt abandoned and betrayed by God; and because he let himself pray what he truly felt, God showed him that He is faithful to who He is and to His promises, even though at the time we might experience Him otherwise.

Because Francis was honest enough to acknowledge his doubt and despair and God's infidelity, as he experienced it, the true God at the center of his heart again rose to the surface of his consciousness to affirm the truth of Francis' perception: God *had* abandoned him, that he might once again give back to God the privilege of being God, independent of Francis, outside his control.

Whatever God deigns to give us of himself is pure gift and not something we earn or deserve by becoming that "perfect" person we think we should be. We are who we are, and any perfection, or completion, in us is the work of God responding freely to our honest prayer that he change in us what we previously thought we could change by ourselves.

Who we become in God is then his work and not our own success in conforming to some ideal. The self we become in true prayer is seldom the self we envisioned, but it is a new and marvelous self that God fashions out of the gradual redeeming of the false self we now acknowledge as the work of our own misguided idealism. We then know God in what he has done in us to enable us to discover our true face. And in that face only do we see the reflection of God as he really is.

7

Prayer and Action

There is a story about Francis' doubt whether he should give himself wholly to prayer or give himself to preaching as well. As in all the important decisions of his life, Francis realizes the danger of self-will and self-deception, and so he seeks the advice of others. He sends Brother Masseo to Brother Sylvester and the Lady Clare that they might ask the Lord in prayer for His will to be made clear.

The focus of this story from *The Little Flowers of St. Francis* is the illusion which everyone faces in the pursuit of God's will: that the life of pure spirit is somehow more perfect than an incarnational life, that it is better to serve God only in prayer than to risk involvement in the lives of others. This is not to say that a life of prayer is an illusion, but that if a life of prayer is really an escape from the complexity of loving others, then I am only seeking to isolate my life in a safe little corner where it cannot be threatened or hurt.

The answer that comes from Sylvester and St. Clare is that Francis should continue preaching to the people; but even if it had been that Francis was to enter wholly into prayer, I believe he would eventually have continued preaching to the people. The reason is that true prayer is never an escape from self but a centering on God, whose face reveals to me my own true face, the face God is summoning forth from my deepest center. And Francis' true face is that of a poor, wandering, *preaching* brother to all of creation.

My suspicion is that Francis already knew God's answer when

he asked for Sylvester's and Clare's advice, but he needed to have confirmed that his preaching was not merely a reaction to his possibly selfish desire to isolate his love life in the love of God. For as soon as Francis heard the answer to his question, he set out immediately to preach, not only to the people, but to the birds as well, thus signifying his involvement with all of creation. The ascent to God begins with the descent into creation, where one participates in the redemption of all creatures by becoming their brother and sister and praising God through them. The core of Francis' prayer is praise and adoration through and for everything that is.

In this way Francis unites prayer and love and puts on the mind of Christ, who ascended to the Father by first descending into creation, taking upon himself our humanity as a model of how we, too, are to return to the Father. And from the life of Jesus, as well as from his own personal experience, Francis knows how messy and complicated the way through creatures is.

It involves the constant draining of your energies, the complexity of interrelating with people, the pain of the death of loved ones and betrayal by your friends. The human dimension becomes so overwhelming that you can no longer see God's face behind the countless masks around you, and you cry out, asking, "Why have you forsaken me?" And it leads to total vulnerability as you hang nailed to your cross, unable to strike back, able only to surrender to the only way to God, the human way that the Son of God Himself chose. It is our humanity crucified by humanity that rises from the dead and ascends to the Father.

Evil is not only something apart from us, but because of the Fall, something within us that makes our suffering inevitable. But because of Jesus Christ, our suffering is redemptive when we surrender to it as an act of union with Him and an act of divine adoration through the humanity which it hurts so much to embrace. That is the prayer, the action which is the way of St. Francis.

8

St. Clare

Clare of Assisi. Of all the great Franciscan saints, she is for me the one most wrapped in mystery. Perhaps it is because she is a contemplative whose inner life is hidden from us except as it is revealed indirectly in her writings. There are volumes of stories about Francis, but very few about Clare, the first woman to join Francis and the brothers.

We know that she was of a noble family and that her sister and eventually her mother, too, joined the Poor Ladies who lived at San Damiano. All her life Clare struggled to preserve what she termed "the privilege of poverty"; and her perseverance was rewarded when on her deathbed she held in her hands a scroll from the Pope granting her and the Poor Ladies of San Damiano the permission to live in perfect gospel poverty, relying wholly on God for their sustenance.

Her relationship with Francis was at first that of a spiritual daughter; and though she continued all her life to call him "our holy Father Francis," she became more than a daughter. Clare emerges as his most faithful companion, the most complete embodiment of the dream and way of life that Francis received from the Lord. She became his partner, the feminine counterpart and complement to the gospel man who follows radically in the footsteps of Christ.

Almost from its very inception the Franciscan life has been infused with both masculine and feminine elements, bringing to the fore the richness of the gospel life or any life when it refuses to be solely masculine or feminine. There is something profoundly womblike about San Damiano and the life that was lived there, as there is something phallic in the brothers' constant forays into the world to preach and witness to the Gospel. I don't think that either venture would have succeeded without the other. The brothers' life on the road enriched the contemplative life of the Poor Ladies; and the ladies' life, in turn, made possible the effectiveness of the brothers' apostolic life and preaching.

The relationship between Francis and Clare and the brothers and Poor Ladies was not something romantic like the relationships of knights and ladies in the tales of courtly love, but they were united by a deep bond of spiritual friendship because of their intense love of Jesus Christ and the common struggle to preserve the gospel ideal of voluntary poverty.

Francis and Clare saw very little of one another, but they each knew the battles and sufferings of the other, and they followed the sacred journey each was making independently yet joined in heart and soul by the call of the Poor Christ which drew them like the legendary Holy Grail.

Francis and Clare were like a new Adam and Eve restoring the decaying Garden of Western Christianity; and though they labored apart, they knew they were never really separated. And this union of heart and soul which was theirs is reflected in art and popular literature from the Middle Ages till now: The story of St. Francis is never complete without St. Clare, nor hers without him. In reality, as well as in the popular mind, the Franciscan life has ever been male and female, and the symbols of that truth are Francis and Clare themselves.

There is a medieval folk tale which not only reveals how their contemporaries viewed Francis and Clare, but which also symbolizes the profound integration of the masculine and feminine in Francis' way to union with God and all of creation. The story appears in Arnaldo Fortini's *Vita Nuova di San Francesco d'Assisi,* which was published in Milan in 1926:

One day Francis and Clare are on a journey together from Spello to Assisi, and on the way they stop and knock at a house for a little bread and water. The family invite them in but proceed to give them suspicious looks and make snide remarks about Francis and Clare being alone together on the road.

The two saints then continue on their way through the snow-felted countryside, for it is winter. And as evening comes on, Francis suddenly says, "Lady Clare, did you understand what the people back there were hinting at?" But Clare is too distressed to answer for fear the words will catch in her throat.

So Francis continues, "It is time for us to part. You will reach San Damiano by nightfall, and I shall go on alone, wherever God leads me."

Then Clare falls to her knees in the middle of the road, prays awhile in silence and walks away without turning around. She walks until she enters a deep wood where she stops, unable to continue without some word of consolation or farewell. So she waits there for Francis; and when he finally enters the wood, she says, "Father, when shall we two meet again?" And Francis replies, "When summer returns and the roses are again in bloom."

Then a miracle occurs: All the surrounding juniper bushes and frosted hedges are covered with roses. And Clare, recovering from her amazement, walks to the bushes and picks a bunch of roses and gives them to Francis.

And so, says the legend, from then on Francis and Clare are never really separate again.

9

The Mirror of St. Clare

Francis met the Lord when he embraced the leper and when he begged for stones and food; and he would never be detoured from that way, because he had found the Lord there. St. Clare finds God in the poverty of contemplation, and she in turn never swerves from *her* way to the end of her life. For Clare poverty and contemplation are so intimately intertwined that contemplation presupposes poverty, because *the Lord promises and gives the Kingdom of Heaven only to the poor.*

As she writes in one of her letters, *What a praiseworthy exchange: to leave temporal things for those that are eternal, to choose heavenly things for earthly goods, to receive a hundredfold instead of one, and to possess a life, blessed and eternal.*

As with Francis, Clare's poverty is not for its own sake but because it makes present the Kingdom and because of *an ardent desire for the Poor Crucified.*

Since the great and good Lord, on entering the Virgin's womb, chose to look despised, needy, and poor in this world, so that people in dire poverty and deprivation and in absolute need of heavenly nourishment might become rich in Him by possessing the Kingdom of Heaven, then you who have chosen poverty should rejoice and be glad!

Always it is the *Poor* Christ whom Clare is determined to gaze upon, consider, and contemplate, because He is the image of God, the Mirror we are to contemplate.

This image of the mirror is central to St. Clare's spirituality. As Francis was the mirror of Christ and Christ of the Father, so the life of the contemplative is to look into the mirror that is Christ and see there oneself, thereby learning who you are. By looking into the mirror who is Christ and recognizing yourself, you become a mirror of Him whom you contemplate, and you in turn mirror, through Christ to the Father, all of creation. You see yourself both *in* a mirror and *as* a mirror.

St. Clare writes to her sisters: *For the Lord Himself has not only placed us as example and mirror for others, but also for our own sisters whom the Lord has called to our way of life, so that they in their turn will be mirror and example to those living in the world.*

This complex imagery shows St. Clare's profound acquaintance with Sacred Scripture, with the literature of the Fathers of the Church, and with the lyrics of the troubadours, all of which are replete with mirror imagery.

There is, for example, a famous twelfth-century version of Ovid's tale of Narcissus in which the troubadour has his Narcissus recognize that he is different from his image in the water, thereby discovering his own separate identity. For a contemplative like St. Clare, however, the birth of self-consciousness through recognition is not enough. She finds her true identity by looking upon Christ and seeing there herself as an image of the Divine; and the more perfectly she mirrors the image of Christ, the more real she becomes. She says in a letter to Blessed Agnes of Prague: *Because the vision of Christ is the splendor of eternal glory, the radiance of eternal light and the mirror without stain, look upon that mirror each day, O queen and spouse of Jesus Christ, and continually study your countenance within it, so that you may clothe yourself inside and out with beautiful robes and cover yourself with the flowers and garments of all the virtues, as becomes the daughter and most chaste bride of the Most High King. Indeed blessed poverty, holy humility, and ineffable charity are reflected in that mirror, and, with the grace of God, you can contemplate them throughout the entire mirror.*

She then expands her imagery to include *the whole mirror. Look at the edges of this mirror, and see the poverty of Him who was placed in a manger and wrapped in swaddling clothes.*

Then looking at the surface of the mirror, dwell on the holy humility, the blessed poverty, the untold labors and burdens which He endured for the redemption of all humankind. Then, in the deep center of the mirror, contemplate the ineffable charity which led Him to suffer on the wood of the Cross, dying on it the most shameful kind of death. Therefore, that Mirror hanging on the wood of the Cross urged those who passed by to consider, saying: "All you who pass by the way, look and see if there is any suffering like My suffering!"

The most striking reality that this imagery confronts us with is the poverty of God. The Poor Christ is the image of the Godhead! God is poor, God is self-emptying; and in our poverty, our resemblance to the poor, crucified Christ, we become mirrors of God Himself. Poverty, then, is not an end in itself, but a way of becoming transformed into an image of the Trinity by contemplating *the* Mirror of the Trinity, Jesus Christ Himself. As a mirror is material yet holds an immaterial image, so the Poor Christ is human and visible yet is an image of the invisible God, who is poor in Triune self-emptying that is simultaneously a filling up.

It is no wonder then that St. Clare holds so tenaciously to contemplation and poverty as a way of life: The two are one: the contemplation of poverty becoming the poverty of contemplation.

10

The Cave

Somehow in middle age many people lose their nerve; they begin to feel that the dream upon which they have based their lives is an illusion. Ours is an anguished age in which the old myths have lost their power and the very virtues which sustained us are warring among themselves. What before was pure and holy now is filled with the impurity of doubt; what before seemed wise and prudent seems now a form of escape, a disengagement from the reality of change and the need to act audaciously and foolishly in order to grow. What began as contemplation has turned out to be a cave full of demons we fled into solitude to escape.

Our prayer does not work because we are afraid to act, to respond to the voice of God crying out for help in the poor and despised, the broken, wounded angels we meet upon our way. In short, we have succumbed to fear and wear God as the mask of respectability that justifies our doing nothing except provide for our security and build protective walls behind which we live the illusion of virtue. We are trying so hard to be safe that we have forgotten how to be human, how to risk, how to dare to live in conflict with the God whose arms alone can wrestle us into life. We no longer dig into the earth to discover what we have inside us; we rape the surface instead, strip-mining for big and fast results. We have abandoned the cave.

Francis, on the other hand, continually returns to the cave. He seeks out lonely places in order to burrow into the earth in search of the treasure which lies hidden from those who live only on the surface. What is this gospel treasure that Francis keeps looking for throughout his life? I believe that it is not so much something hidden in the earth as it is something hidden in the self that you discover in the process of burrowing in the ground, something you discover about yourself.

For Francis, as for the epic hero, the cave is the repository of some intangible Grail that lies in wait for one who is brave enough to dig for it. Always some monster is guarding the treasure, challenging the hero to overcome the fear of harm and death, to do battle with the demonic creature who dwells not in the earth but in the depths of the soul. The cave is symbolic, relating the soul to its own dark depths and to the archeology of humankind as well. The prize is not some priceless possession but the resurrection that occurs in the pursuer's soul, a new wholeness, a further integration that is effected each time one enters the cave of the self to do battle with the demon of fear.

That we lose our nerve in middle age, or any other age, is not necessarily something negative. It can be the voice of our own depths summoning us again to descend and, in descending, to discover the reasons for that uneasiness that continues to surface, paralyzing us and keeping us from walking upright. Union with God and our fellow human beings is effected in the depths of our own selves where we are reconciled with ourselves, where we "surrender" to our humanity by wrestling with those demons that are preventing us from being human and thereby from being united with God and others as whole persons.

We are open to the Divine only to the extent that we are open to our own humanity, only to the extent that we are who we are, and not some purely spiritual beings denying the dust from which we were fashioned and into which God breathed His own Spirit. Only soul *and* body can become spirit, and their union takes place deep inside where our humanity waits for the wrestling that becomes embrace, transforming what was the enemy into the spouse. From this marriage the whole person emerges whom God impregnates with His Spirit. That is what asceticism is all about, what it means to lead a life of union with God and others, and it can all begin with disillusionment or a simple loss of nerve.

11

Francis and the Cave Dwellers

Once upon a very dark time there was a young dreamer from Assisi who fell in love with the real Jesus-mystery of God's love for him.

And he discovered as soon as he left the feather beds and velvet curtains of home that life is a journey not so much outward and away as inward toward the core of the heart and then outward through the heart and that caves are best for that kind of journey.

In the dark cave of himself he found no reflections of the world outside or of the ideal world but only darkness and dampness and the self-sweat of fear.

And out of the cave emerged a Francis so accustomed to the dark that all light was bright to him and the world was ever shining and shimmering with sunbeams and moonbeams and fireflies and stars.

And he walked in the light all the days of his life, singing for joy that there are more outside places than inside places, and if one is ever to enjoy the outside of the world, he first has to climb down inside and stumble around there for a while.

And he loved the birds because there were no birds in the caves of Umbria, except bats, and they were the kind of birds you would become if you never left the cave in daylight but waited till the earth was dark to show yourself.

And Francis learned from the bats in his cave that you can't fly when you cling desperately to the roofs of caves and you have to hang upside down to do it and you get a puffy little face with bulging eyeballs like a bat's and you fly all alone and jerkily and you scare people and they run away from you.

So Francis decided he'd have to escape from solid things like caves and be poor and not cling to anything that would keep him from flying in the daytime brilliance of the Umbrian countryside, and he would not fly alone but with other bright birds and they would celebrate the blue, cloudless skies of freedom together.

And the Poor Savior charmed him and he didn't know how he was ever going to return so much love if not by heralding Christ to the world as the first human to escape the cave forever.

And Francis became the liberator of cave dwellers all over the world by shining the resurrected Christ into dark caves for all time to come.

12

Obedience

Unlike an obsessive love for another human being, which can result in a loss of self-identity, the total love of God brings with it a strengthening of a sense of self, a serene clarification of who I am. Francis loved God with a radical intensity; yet far from losing himself, he became one of the most clearly defined individuals in history, a man so unique that his life is the stuff of legend and myth. In losing himself in God, Francis discovers who he really is: a child of God and a brother to all of creation, especially to those lowly men and women with whom Jesus identified himself and whose love cost Him His life.

One of the strangest stories about Francis is his comparison of the obedient person to a corpse. *He is sitting with his companions, and he says something like this: "There is hardly a friar in the whole world who obeys perfectly." Taken aback, his brothers say to him: "Tell us, Father, what is the perfect and highest obedience." And Francis replies, using the figure of a corpse to describe the truly obedient person. "Take a corpse and place it wherever you want. You will see that it doesn't resist being moved, it doesn't complain about its position, it doesn't cry out if it is allowed to lie there. If it is placed on a chair, it won't look up but down; if it is clothed in purple, it looks twice as pale. This is true obedience: not to ask why you are moved, not to care where you are placed, not to insist on being changed somewhere else. Raised to an office, you retain your accustomed humility; the more you are honored, the more unworthy you consider yourself."*

Like so many of the Francis stories, this one has to be read from the viewpoint of Francis himself and how he thought. Behind this story is the story of Paradise, in which obedience is joined to life and disobedience to death. In choosing what they thought was life, Adam and Eve were really choosing death, a mistake repeated all through the ages by the person who sees with the eyes and hears with the ears of the flesh.

The obedient person, on the other hand, seems to be choosing death, seems even corpselike in his or her response; but paradoxically, in choosing what seems to be death, he or she is really choosing life. Disobedience seeking life brought death into the world; obedience that seems to be death-seeking brings life. It is the story of Adam mistakenly choosing death through life and Jesus choosing life and becoming Life through death, thereby restoring and again opening to us the Garden of Paradise.

There is, I think, a further implication in Francis' story. As only the Spirit can give true life to body and soul, and without it they are only seemingly alive, so only obedience to God can raise the person to true life in the Spirit. Obedience is a paradigm of martyrdom, because like martyrdom it seems to be a foolish choosing of death whereas it is really the fullness of life, the highest identification with the obedient Lamb of God, Jesus Christ, whose own martyrdom was an act of obedience to the Father that brought life to the world. The image behind the corpse of obedience is the Lamb led to slaughter.

And as martyrdom is surrender to Love through other people acting as God's instruments, so obedience is really to God through his ministers. In both cases God acts through those invested with authority, and in both cases these human instruments seem to be nothing more than executioners, dealing death rather than life, like Abraham standing, knife in hand, over his son Isaac.

In Francis' thinking, obedience is always associated with martyrdom: Neither can be chosen merely through will power; they are acts of the Spirit. The story above, for example, is followed by these words: *But Francis thought it the highest obedience and without anything of flesh and blood when one goes by divine inspiration among the infidels, either for one's neighbor's sake or out of a desire for martyrdom. He thought it highly acceptable to God to ask for this obedience.*

Such a statement dispels the danger inherent in the corpse image which Francis uses: that misreading of the story which interprets it to mean that the best way to God is to fold your hands and, refusing to take responsibility for your life, allow others to make your decisions for you. Such a passive, dependent stance is not at all what Francis means in comparing the obedient person to a corpse, for no immature person would ever ask to be sent into danger in order to be martyred; rather he or she would avoid all danger by becoming wholly submissive to another, thereby insuring one's safety. For who would send another to martyrdom or even into danger unless he or she asked to be sent?

The emphasis of Francis is on asking, on choosing, to become obedient as a corpse, which is quite different from being submissive because you are afraid to choose, afraid to assert yourself. The truly holy person chooses obedience the way a knight rides purposefully into battle, or like Christ, who emptied Himself, taking the form of a slave, not because He was weak, but because he chose to do so in order to become one with us. Obedience, embraced for the right reason, makes us one with all of creation, because it makes us one with Christ who is the Firstborn of all creatures.

13

Father and Son

I

The Francis who bends tenderly over the humblest creature, blessing it and speaking to it is at root the same Francis who rode off to war to slaughter others, the same Francis who violently renounces his father before the Bishop of Assisi, a decision that must have appeared to some onlookers like an impetuous, headstrong move that went further than Francis had intended; but true son of Pietro Bernardone that he was, he had to save face and not back off. That was not the whole of what happened, but I believe there are elements of truth in this impression of the townspeople.

Francis *is* the son of Pietro Bernardone, and no decision to call only God his father can change that. The placid son of God is also the volcanic son of Bernardone. There is a little passage in *The Legend of the Three Companions* that is a revealing portrait of both father and son. The context is Pietro's reaction to Francis' dressing in a hermit's garment and living at San Damiano and begging stones for the run-down chapel.

When Pietro saw Francis' miserable plight, he was very sad, for he loved him dearly; he was grieved and ashamed to see his son half dead from penance and hardships, and whenever they met, he cursed Francis.

This brief passage reminds me of Francis himself before the Bishop of Assisi. I believe you could change a few words and have a fairly accurate portrait of Francis himself: *When Francis saw Pietro's miserable plight, he was very sad, for he loved him dearly; he was grieved and ashamed to see his father half dead from his obsession with money and power. And when he met his father in the bishop's piazza, he renounced him publicly.*

Neither man is given to hesitation and timidity; neither is guarded of his feelings; both are dramatic, violent men.

A whole other story of Francis is contained in his relationship with his father and the ineffectiveness of his mother's place between them. Everything that Francis' mother and/or father did for him only left him feeling emotionally abandoned by them. His mother was too weak to provide a buffer between Francis and his father's wrath, and his father refused to listen or even try to understand. All Pietro could do was curse, and all Francis could do was counterattack with rejection: *When he heard his father's curses, he took as father a poor and hated outcast and said to him, "Come with me and I will give you the alms I receive; and when I hear my father cursing me, I'll turn to you and say, 'Bless me, Father'; and then you sign me with the cross and bless me in his stead." And the next time Pietro cursed his son, the beggar blessed him; and Francis turned to his father and said, "Don't you realize that God can give me a father with blessings to counter your curses?"*

It is not hatred that moves Pietro to curse his son, but love. Because he is not open to anything but his own image of what his son should be and his own plans for him, he is filled with frustration and rage that Francis, in becoming his own man, in growing up, as he should, is bringing shame on his father who loves him. Pietro has been publicly disgraced by his son's behavior, and he cannot understand how Francis could do this to him.

Francis, for his part, sees how imprisoned his father is by respectability and the need to preserve appearances at all costs. And Francis again reacts: *Meanwhile he kept working steadily at restoring the church of San Damiano, and because he wanted the sanctuary light to be kept burning, he begged through the city for oil. Once, when he came to a particular house, he saw some men busy playing and gambling; overcome by shyness, he turned away, ashamed to go in and beg from them. But then he changed his mind, and accusing himself of sin, hurried back to the house, went in, and confessed to all the company that he had been ashamed to ask them for alms.*

Nothing could have hurt Pietro more than Francis' need to overcome shame by submitting to shame, and thereby submitting the family to the disgrace of his begging.

It is hard for us to understand what Francis is doing here because most of us, like Pietro, recoil from anguish and take refuge in retreat. Francis does not. He always faces the truth of his present, no matter what the consequences might be.

There is in the above incident a further dimension beyond the tension in the relationship between Francis and his father. Francis strikes at the heart of the hypocrisy of his world, a world for whom reputation and good name is more important than goodness and truth, a world in which people commit suicide when their reputation is under fire; and their reputation is to be equated with their identity and their identity with success, financial and social.

In choosing "failure" from the outset, Francis frees himself from the enormous burden of the opinion of others. Beginning with his own father, he rejects knowing who he is only through others. He becomes a free man, a man whose identity comes from God.

Most of us spend our lives trying to make this kind of break, suffering because we cannot, developing anxieties and phobias, surrendering finally to the general mediocrity; sad, a bit bitter, surrounding ourselves with small successes that don't quite make us forget our great defeat. We know instinctively that Francis' ability to act where most would hesitate is his greatness. His is the great leap through absurdity to faith. He chooses *what is foolish in the world to shame the wise, . . . what is weak in the world to shame the strong, . . . what is low and despised in the world, even things that are not, to bring to nothing things that are, so that no human being might boast in the presence of God.* (1 Cor. 1:27–28)

In rejecting his earthly father, Francis simultaneously embraces his Heavenly Father, thus escaping the terrible trauma of complete alienation, of not belonging anywhere, of being alone. Francis' new identity comes from God. And he begins almost immediately to recognize his father and mother and brothers and sisters as those who do the will of his Father in Heaven. He develops a whole new sense of family.

II

Somehow God becomes the face of one's deepest desire, and the most significant moments of life alter the face of God. I believe that for Francis the face of God was, at the beginning, the face of his mother, Lady Pica, and at the end, the face of his father, Pietro. For the deepest unfulfilled desire of his heart was that he and his father would be reconciled. I say "unfulfilled" because there is no historical evidence that Pietro and his son were ever reconciled after that terrible scene before the bishop when Francis renounces his father.

From my thirteenth year, when I read my first biography of St. Francis, I have felt pity for Pietro and puzzlement at Francis that he, the saint, apparently went down to his grave without making peace with his father.

Was this, as some have suggested, because Francis took the Gospel literally and believed he must leave father and mother irrevocably in order to belong wholly to Christ? Or was the reconciliation of father and son omitted by the early hagiographers as inconsequential to the life of one who stepped boldly in the footsteps of Christ? The latter seems hardly plausible: that such a profoundly Christlike act should be omitted from the life of the great peacemaker of the Middle Ages. And the former is too simplistic an answer for a sensitive person like Francis.

I believe the answer is as complicated as the relationship between father and son, as full of paradox as the Gospel. And though I have already touched on Francis and his father, I would like to dwell further on their relationship, because I believe it is central to an understanding of Francis and his image of God.

No matter how famous Francis became, how revered as a saint, he remained always son to Pietro, his words to the contrary notwithstanding. And though he could preach to others, and even to the birds, with astonishing effect, it would have been an affront to his father to confront him with the Gospel of love after so humiliating him that day when he was very young and brash and filled with the self-righteousness of the newly born into Christ.

Had Francis remained rejected and despised, as he was at the beginning of his conversion, it is conceivable that he could have come to his father and begged his forgiveness for shaming him in public and asked him to try to understand the sincerity of his decision to serve God alone. But once he became "Il Santo," the saint of Assisi, he could never have begged Pietro's forgiveness without further humiliating his father and making him an object of pity for failing to see how great a prophet his son really was.

I want to believe that a secret reconciliation did take place, that Francis comforted his dying father and received his blessing; but that is likely only something inside myself that needs it to have happened that way. Experience and the testimony of his chroniclers tell me it was otherwise: that the Gospel divides families, that mothers lose their sons because of their husbands, and sons reject their fathers because of their own call to be themselves, to be different from the one who engendered them. And God's face becomes the face of what each one wishes secretly could have happened, had not pride or circumstances or life itself made it impossible.

14

A Ceremony of Investiture

Behind much of Francis' public behavior is the fact that he *is* a *public* personality, a man who has done what he has done before the whole city of Assisi. He has renounced his father in front of the assembled citizens; he, the wealthy merchant's son, has begged in the streets; those who joined him openly gave away their money and possessions in the town square. Francis was a public witness to the Gospel, and those who followed him were very much aware of the public nature of their vocation.

But there was more than a certain visibility and notoriety involved in the Franciscan vocation. Like the great investiture ceremonies of ancient mythology and of knighthood, the decision to embrace Lady Poverty and follow in the footsteps of Christ was indeed a true investiture that stripped the brothers and sisters of their private character and clothed them in the vestment of their vocation. No longer were they responsible only to themselves for themselves, but now they were responsible to society, with whom they had made a solemn contract. As Francis used to say, *There is a contract between the world and the brothers: The brothers must give the world a good example; the world must provide for their needs. When the brothers break faith and withdraw their good example, the world will withdraw its hand in just censure.*

The brothers and the Poor Ladies of San Damiano had ceased to be private persons only. Like the heroes and heroines of mythology, their investiture defined their place in society and defined their personal relationship to it. This is one of the rea-

sons for Francis' strong language against leaving the brotherhood: *It is absolutely forbidden to leave the Order, as his holiness the Pope has decreed. For the Gospel says, "No one having
put his hand to the plough and looking back, is fit for the
kingdom of God."* (Lk. 9:62)

What the brothers and Poor Ladies had done outwardly had
been a profound inner action as well. They had cut the umbili-
cal cord of the mother and been born again into the larger
family, society. To return to their former lives is to return to the
womb, a denial of vocation, of the quest, in favor of nurturing
the self; and the harmony of the one and the many is broken.

Today, when the validity of traditional mythologies is ques-
tioned and the unconscious life of the individual is what is
probed and invested with great importance, the ideal is harmony between the conscious and unconscious life rather than
between the self and the myth. But at the same time, one of the
great breakthroughs of modern psychology is the discovery that
the archetypes and symbols of mythology and religion are also
those that rise spontaneously from the unconscious. Nor is this
discovery surprising given the fact that religions and myths do
not arise out of a vacuum; the gods have always spoken through
the unconscious, and myths are really projections of the great
symbols and movements of the gods within and upon the unconscious.

For a medieval poet and mythmaker like Francis the refusal
of a vocation is the denial of the movement of God in one's life, a
rejection of the bond with that Someone within and apart from
me who called me and to whom I responded. In His presence I
call upon society to witness and ratify what I have done, since
my vocation is what defines for others how I relate to them.

Then what about those today who leave the Religious life and
return to the world? Are they, as some maintain, regressing to
an infantile state of dependence upon another, who then becomes "mother" or "father" for them? Such a simplistic view
overlooks the mystery of our mythology, both personal and
collective, or tries to control it and understand it by labeling
and pigeonholing and explaining. My own presumption is in
favor of the individual—that what one does vis-à-vis vocation is

not done lightly and usually derives from a deeper, closer awareness of one's inner movement, both conscious and unconscious.

For what you embrace on the conscious level, if it does not correspond to who you are on the unconscious level, is really an acting out of what you think others expect of you or what you expect of yourself. Then when you one day come to grips with your true movement from the depths of who you are, you see that what you have initially committed yourself to is an action of the superficial you and not of the whole self in touch with who it really is. And you are impelled from within to become the self you have denied; and this involves either a new, more realistic commitment to your previous response, or a rejection of your first response as having been made without knowing who you really were. You discover that God speaks from within as well as calls from without.

We are all subject to self-deception, of course, but who is to judge that for anyone but oneself? I prefer to believe that in leaving one vocation for another, the individual has finally found his or her true self.

15

Intimacy

I

Images begin to move in my mind, and there on the white screen is Francis and the snow people. He is *gathering handfuls of snow and making from it seven snowballs.*

And setting them in front of him, he starts to speak to his body. "There now, this stouter one is your wife; these four are your two sons and your two daughters; the other two are your servant and your maid. Go ahead now, Francis, clothe them all; you can see they are dying of cold. But if caring for them like this troubles you, be concerned about serving God alone."

Was it humor only that moved him to build a snow family when the ache of intimacy was upon him? Was it the humor that diffuses passion that moved him to speak to his snow creatures? Or was it something more, a realization that they could not survive outside his fantasy, out there in the real snow he could touch and address, the snow that was only snow?

His wife and children were really those who walked with him up the mountain, their eyes fixed on the peak of their own vision, hearing their separate calls from God. They walked the same road as a family because they had the same Father. They were brothers and sisters, and they did not need each other as spouses to satisfy their longing for intimacy; they were already, men and women both, brides of Christ. Every other spouse was for Francis a mirage in the snow that he had to dispel by building snow people who let him see how fantasy melts away outside the mind.

There is something very charming and true about this story and yet so unsatisfying for those of us who are not saints, who lead divided lives. Francis' gesture does not help where we most need help, in the center of the heart divided by compromises and by loves other than God. The story of the seven snow people is too easy, too quick a solution to the conflict that splits the hearts of many who want to love God above all else and yet keep finding that He is most real in the human loves of their lives, loves that do not dissolve like snow people, loves they cannot walk away from like some creation of their own hands that is a projection of their desires.

So often these loves are not sought, not created, but come to us as gifts or challenges. And they involve us over and over in choices we do not want to make—choices like divine or human love, God or this human being. And so we compromise and try to render to each his or her due, wondering if either God or the human receives their due from us who are divided in our giving, hedging always, unwilling to abandon love for Love, not knowing even if we should.

Somewhere deep inside we know that love is not an either/or decision but a giving and receiving full of confusion and pain: still, a giving and receiving nonetheless, a mutuality that succeeds, if at all, only in not being wholly self-serving in the end. The truth is that all vows are compromised one way or another, be they marriage vows or religious vows, because nothing is totally pure or clear-cut. We live the mystery of good and evil; and out of the struggle within that mystery, we learn who we are and how it is we give and receive, according to our own measure and according to the amount of ambiguity we can tolerate.

It can be a very selfish thing to love God alone, as it can be an illusion to love Him only through others. But neither God nor people are served by our love of one to the exclusion of the other. True love is inclusive, and God and the human are one in the Incarnation. Even in Jesus, the Divine and the human were in conflict: *Father, if it is your will, let this cup pass from me; yet not my will but yours be done.* (Lk. 22:42) The human in Jesus surrenders to the Divine but not without conflict, not without thinking he had failed to retain his hold on the Divine; *My God, my God, why have you forsaken me?* (Mk. 15:34)

The story of the seven snow people has always troubled me because the conflict seems contrived, invented almost, to show how single-minded a saint must be. Someone left the heart out of the story in his zeal to keep Francis above the rest of us. Yet how different is God's storytelling, how lacking in pious icing. He does not dawdle with creatures of snow but through Hosea, the prophet, He says: *Go, take a harlot wife and harlot's children, for the land gives itself to harlotry, turning away from the Lord. . . . Give your love to a woman beloved of a paramour, an adultress; Even as the Lord loves the people of Israel, though they turn to other gods and are fond of raisin cakes.* (Hos. 1:2, 3:1–2)

What a bizarre request! And yet this is the God Francis loves over his own father, both of them asking impossible things of him, but his Heavenly Father more honest, more real to Francis because He is the Father of the Word. It is the Father of Jesus whom Francis loves, the Father who raises up our failure and after three days redeems His Word that He loves us with an everlasting love.

The Father revealed by Jesus is the Father who rises from Francis' loins, the Father that Pietro Bernardone, or any earthly father, cannot be. He is antecedent to all fatherhood and His claim supersedes whatever claim an earthly father might have. His demands are individual to each person and sometimes seem capricious in the cup He asks us to drink. From the same God can come the request to renounce the love of any woman or man, or the request to marry a harlot.

What He asks of us is often an image of where His people are and how they love or do not love Him at a given time. Our human loving is a mirror of our love of God. For us to try to love God medievally is to live an unreal life. He speaks to us through our present loving to correct and inspire, to redeem and make whole again.

We are not to squander our time looking for ideal loves; we

are to love those the Lord has given us. And we become holy by really or symbolically laying down our lives for them as Jesus did for us.

The desire to simplify our lives and draw close to God can be nothing more than the desire to escape the cross of a difficult love, a love that is draining and unfulfilling. And instead of walking the road to the final revelation of Emmaus, where Christ is revealed in the breaking of the bread that we have become, we turn away from being bread broken and consumed; we look desperately for shortcuts and ways back to a simpler, less complicated life.

II

In trying to discover if Francis has anything to say to us about intimacy, it was still not clear until I came upon this passage in Thomas of Celano's *Second Life of Francis*. Francis says, *Our greatest enemy is the flesh*. But then he defines what he means by "flesh."

It does not know how to remember anything to repent over it; it does not know how to foresee consequences to fear them; its sole aim is to misuse the present time; but what is worse, it claims as its own, and for its own glory what belongs to the soul. It seeks praise for its virtues and the superficial favor of others for its vigils and prayers. It leaves nothing for the soul, but seeks to be rewarded even for its tears. For Francis the flesh has no sense of the past or of the future, and it misuses the present. It is the great appropriator, the archenemy of poverty.

In Francis' mind *appropriation* is the great sin because it claims for self what really belongs to God, who has lent us whatever we have. Whenever Francis received praise, he would say, *If he who lent me these things should ever wish to take them back, only body and soul would remain, and these even the unbeliever possesses.*

It is when we attribute to ourselves and try to hold onto what is in reality God's gift that we are of the flesh, appropriators who violate holy poverty. For Francis, then, everything revolves around poverty. And insofar as anything appropriates to itself what really belongs to God or another, it is of the flesh. The poor person of the Gospel appropriates nothing. There is affectivity and warmth in poverty, but intimacy implies for Francis an appropriation of that which he has relinquished in order that through dispossession he might possess the Lord.

How different that is from the fear of women or men, or that unbalanced fear of the body as evil, or worse, as the creation of the Evil One. Francis' way is the way of the pilgrim, and the only home he has is the brotherhood itself; the only intimacy, the embrace of God.

III

The word "flesh" is a troublesome word because we have come to equate it with "body," which is not what it means at all. True asceticism is not a holy warfare between the body and the soul, but a battle between flesh and spirit, which are biblical terms for *tendencies which inform and shape* both *body and soul. "Spirit" is an orientation toward union with the source of life and being; "flesh" is a disorientation away from this source, the desperate and unconscious demand for immediate satisfactions that can overpower body and soul and leave them unfree and uncentered. The flesh's domination robs soul and body of their true vitality.*

Because we have come to associate flesh with body, we automatically think that our evil tendencies, our disorientations, stem from the body, which is not true and certainly not the way St. Francis thought. It is the flesh which disorients, which is the source of sin, and the flesh affects both the soul and the body. Francis' whole asceticism is an endeavor to become a man of the spirit rather than of the flesh, and it is not an endeavor to rid himself of his body that he might become pure soul. You lose body and soul when you are obedient to the flesh, you save them both when you are obedient to the spirit.

Given the fact that flesh is not body and spirit is not soul, and that the real battle in Francis' life is between flesh and spirit and not body and soul, still there is in Francis a violence toward his own body that makes one think that he saw his own body as the source of evil in his life. He was so hard on his own body that toward the end of his life he apologized to it and called his body affectionately *Brother Ass.*

How, then, can Francis' extreme penances and mortification be explained? Did he see the body as innately blind and selfish, the most tangible expression of what is grasping and possessive, bent solely on its own gratification? Were his penances concrete expressions of the mastery of will over instinct, spirit over flesh? Or was there something deeper at work?

I don't think it is possible to separate Francis' penances from his love of Jesus Christ crucified. So radical is Francis' love of Christ that he wants to experience the pain of the Beloved, to be so identified with Christ that he knows "from the inside" what Jesus suffered. Furthermore he is bent on loving God with his whole soul and heart and mind, but his wayward heart keeps revealing itself in the "selfish" demands of his own body.

All of this seems at best unbalanced to the "sensible" person. It makes God look punitive and cruel, asking us to suppress and deny and beat down every natural and spontaneous human drive and desire. And in one sense Francis appears unreasonable to those of us less smitten. He is a hero in love, his language and actions those of a person whose heart has been wounded by love, who is intoxicated by the perfume of the Beloved. To others the heroic lover always seems a bit mad, someone going through a phase, someone who will eventually pass from the insanity of *being in love* to the sanity and reasonableness of *love*. But that does not happen to Francis. He is in love with Jesus Christ all his life, like a young lover who is experiencing for the first time what it means to fall in love.

Francis' commitment to and love of God is so great that he reacts violently whenever his deep desire for human intimacy or union with someone other than God manifests itself through his own body. He punishes his body for responding to the flesh that he is struggling to overcome. He is trying to surrender soul and body to the spirit, and the violence of the struggle is made manifest in his physical punishment of the stubborn, intransigent *Brother Ass.*

But always it is love which is Francis' motivation, not self-hatred. It is the love of the mystic, the love so beautifully expressed by the Franciscan poet Jacopone da Todi: *Love, love, my heart is so broken; love, love, I am so wounded. Love, love, your beauty draws me to you; love, love, I am fully enwrapped in you. Love, love, I disdain to live; love, love, my spirit is united with you. Love, you are its life and it cannot be separated from you. Love, why do you make it languish, hugging you so?*

Love, love, desired Jesus, I want to die embracing you. Love, love, Jesus, my sweet spouse; love, love, I ask death of you. Love, love, Jesus so delightful, you give yourself to me, transforming me into you. I think I will faint. Love, I don't know where I am. Jesus, my hope, cast me into the abyss of love.

IV

It is through a life vowed to God that Francis achieves the intimacy that eluded him when he was a young man of the world. This is something that I have guessed for years, but only in my own struggles with intimacy and in writing these pages has its truth come clear. The way of life Francis gave me has enabled me to know a real intimacy with God, with people, and with all of creation. To reach for an intimacy beyond the vows one has made is to misunderstand the nature of the vowed life itself and the intimacy already effected in what you have promised to observe. There is a great mystery here, but I believe that at the very heart of poverty, chastity, and obedience is the union so sought after elsewhere in our lives.

The gospel life purifies the roots of love and transforms poverty into a lady who, like Dante's Beatrice, leads us into God; obedience is transformed into a profound entering into creatures where we see anew and proclaim:

I find you, Lord in all things in all
my fellow creatures, pulsing with your life;
as a tiny seed you sleep in what is small
and in the vast you vastly yield yourself.

The wondrous game that power plays with things
is to move in such submission through the world:
groping in roots and growing thick in trunks
and in treetops like a rising from the dead.

And chastity becomes a generativity and fruitfulness that makes us *spouses and mothers of our Lord Jesus Christ.*

It is almost half a year since I wrote the tortured sentences about Francis and the snow people, and my summer words seem overblown and out of proportion now, as if I'd given intimacy a centrality it does not deserve and a place in Francis' life that belongs to God alone. As it does in life, so on the page, the search for intimacy can usurp the search for God. The trouble is, God is not "out there" but within, enfleshed in human beings; and so the old question returns and intimacy with God wears again a human face.

It is the Incarnation itself which gives intimacy its theological importance, but with the modern preoccupation with sexuality, the word "intimacy" has certain overtones and creates expectations which the experience of intimacy may or may not contain. Just as sexual activity does not necessarily include intimacy, so intimacy need not include sexual activity. What intimacy does include is our sexuality itself, our maleness and/or femaleness. We love God and people as men and women, not as sexless automatons. And the only restrictions to our loving are God's command to love Him and our neighbor as ourselves and the promises we have made to Him and/or another human being. Common sense and our own good heart usually supply the rest.

We moderns reach down deep within ourselves to discover who we are; medievals like St. Francis look into the mirror of creation or into themselves as mirrors of the Creator to know who they are. They see reflections of themselves in nature and reflections of God in themselves. Their world is platonic, reflecting the ideal forms of heaven. The snow people Francis makes are mirrors of the craziness of his fantasies, given the promises he has made to the Lord.

But perhaps the most significant factor in Francis' rejection of his snow wife is his love for another woman, the illusive Lady

Poverty. This woman, who rose from the depths of his own unconscious, pointed the way to a life that he had hitherto not even imagined. She is always just ahead, appearing and disappearing from sight. She cannot be possessed, because she is the personification of dispossession. She is the way and the destination, the consummation and the deprivation simultaneously. And her voice, deep within Francis, beckons him ever on into God by a way already imprinted with the footsteps of her first lovers: *I was once in the Paradise of my God, where people walked naked; in fact, I walked in them and with them in their nakedness throughout that most splendid Paradise, fearing nothing, doubting nothing, and suspecting no evil. I thought that I would be with them forever, for the Most High created them just, good, and wise and placed them in that pleasant and beautiful place. I rejoiced exceedingly and played before them all the while, for possessing nothing, they belonged entirely to God.*

But then evil entered the garden and we fell from innocence, and the Lady Poverty became a fugitive upon the earth. *From then on I did not find a resting place for my foot. While Abraham, Isaac, and Jacob, and the rest received in promise riches and a land flowing with milk and honey, I sought rest in them and did not find it until the Most High came into the world from the bosom of the Father, he who in his graciousness sought me out.*

It is Jesus Himself, then, who becomes Lady Poverty's true spouse, as the brothers themselves describe when they tell her why they, too, love her and seek her out all the days of their lives: *Thus it was that the Son of the Most High Father became enamored of your beauty; while he was in the world, he clung to you alone and proved that you were completely faithful in everything. And you, a most faithful spouse, a most tender lover, did not for one moment abandon him; what is more, you clung to him even more faithfully the more you saw him despised by all others. But, of course, if you had not been with him, he could never have been so despised. In the end, when he went to heaven, he left to you the seal of the Kingdom of Heaven to use in sealing the elect. Then whoever would sigh for the eternal Kingdom would have to come to you to beg it from you and enter it through you, for no one can enter into the Kingdom unless sealed with your seal.*

Lady Poverty's response to the friars becomes *the* reason for Francis' celibacy and why he considered even a wife and children an appropriation. To follow in the footsteps of Christ meant to walk as he did without anything or anyone to call his own: *Before the Most High returned to his Father who had sent him, he left a testament to the faithful concerning me: Do not keep gold or silver, or money.* (Mt. 10:9) *Take nothing for your journey, neither a bag nor a wallet nor bread nor a staff nor shoes; neither have two tunics.* (Mt. 10:10; Mk. 6:8; Lk. 9:3) *And if anyone would go to law with you and take your tunic, let him take your cloak as well; and whoever forces you to go for one mile, go with him two.* (Mt. 5:40–41)

Do not lay up for yourselves treasures on earth, where rust and moth consume, and where thieves break in and steal. (Mt. 6:19) *Do not be anxious, saying, "What shall we eat?" or "What shall we drink?" or "What are we to put on?"* (Mt. 6:31) *Do not be anxious about tomorrow, for tomorrow will have anxieties of its own. Sufficient for the day is its own trouble.* (Mt. 6:34) *Everyone of you who does not renounce all that he possesses cannot be my disciple.* (Lk. 14:33)

These passages from Scripture become the brothers' words of betrothal to Lady Poverty, and what does not conform literally to them becomes a mere figure of snow that melts before the sun of justice and truth.

V

For Francis the fullness of humanity is expressed in the self-emptying of Jesus, so that the paradox of emptiness that is fullness is made tangible in the human God, Jesus Christ.

The mysticism of St. Francis is centered on the humanity of Christ, which is most evident in His being born of a human mother and in His death upon the Cross. These two events are at the center of Francis' spirituality.

In fact, it is from Francis' intense love of the God who was born and died for us that we have Christmas cribs and crucifixes portraying the human, suffering Jesus; it is because of him that artists began to see and paint a very human Mary nursing a real baby instead of a stylized Christ child; and it is because of his intense love of the crucified Christ that Francis himself is imprinted with the wounds of Christ, the sacred stigmata.

All of this is to say that Francis' life was filled with intimacy, but it was an intimacy with God that in imitation of Jesus was a self-emptying. Francis refused to cling to human intimacy so that he might become more intimate with God, as God had refused to cling to His Divinity in order to become intimate with us. Francis discovered that for Jesus birth is death and death is birth, and that paradox became the motivating truth behind everything that we find seemingly contradictory in Francis' life.

A further deepening of his living of the Christian mystery was Francis' embodiment of the paradox that birth is both life *and* death, as death is both death *and* life. Like Jesus in whose footsteps he walked, Francis is a sign of contradiction, and there are certain things in his life that can only be understood in light of the profound paradox of the self-emptying God.

This self-emptying God, this Jesus Christ, is the object of Francis' total love. Francis is in love with God, but because this God is also human, in loving Him Francis is in love with everything it means to be human. When Francis prays, *My God and my all,* the God he addresses is He who "did not think to snatch at equality with God, but made himself nothing, assuming the nature of a slave. Bearing the human likeness, revealed in human shape, he humbled himself, and in obedience accepted even death—death on a cross." (Phil. 2:6–8)

Jesus Christ is so real to Francis and his love for Him so personal that intimacy with anyone else is a betrayal of that love. It is not that he loves God and rejects humanity, but because the God he loves is human as well as divine, to love intimately another human being would be an infidelity and a violation of the vows of poverty, chastity, and obedience, all three of which wed Francis to Jesus Christ.

In my mind the attitude of Francis toward women is akin to

that of Mary toward Joseph. Mary does not make love with Joseph, not because there is something intrinsically evil about sexual intimacy, something unworthy of the Mother of God, but because she is already married to the Holy Spirit and is pregnant by Him with Jesus. So also with Francis. His relationship with Jesus is as intimate as that of brother and mother *and spouse: Oh, how glorious it is, how holy and great, to have a Father in heaven! Oh, how holy, consoling, beautiful and wondrous it is to have such a Spouse! Oh, how holy and how loving, pleasing, humble, peaceful, sweet, lovable, and desirable above all things to have such a Brother and such a Son.*

The language of intimacy in these lines from Francis' *Letter to the Faithful* is almost staggering in its intensity. God is lover, brother, and son; we make love with Him in the Spirit, we are born from the same womb as He, and we even bring Him to birth within us. Francis' words are filled with generativity, with womb, and there is nothing of deprivation or sterility in his relationship with God.

And this is where my journey with Francis has led. He who is my Vergil has become my Beatrice as well, leading me into my own loins become womb, where I am lover, brother, mother to the God I thought was somewhere "out there," like a spire erectile against the sky. God is womb and in Him alone is intimacy whole—human *and* divine.

16

The Exchange of Love

Although Francis related to the brothers as a brother, they always looked to him as more than that. He was their "father," and in his writings and admonitions Francis is always father, gently leading his brothers to their true Father in heaven.

What Francis sought most of all was to follow in the footsteps of Jesus Christ and in so doing to draw with him those whom the Lord had entrusted to his care. It was a way the Lord Himself had shown him, not a way others had charted out beforehand. *When God gave me some brothers, there was no one to tell me what I was to do; but the Most High himself made it plain to me that I must live the life of the Gospel.*

And the Rule he drew up was not a set of do's and don'ts that regulated every little detail of the brothers' lives. Rather it was only an exterior framework by which, in the spirit of freedom, the brothers could find and follow the footsteps of Jesus Christ. The followers of Francis were not "conforming" to a set of rules so much as embracing a way within which they could live the Gospel in that purity of heart which is *always searching for heavenly things, never failing to keep God before their eyes and always adoring him with a pure heart and soul.*

The *Rule of 1223* is simple and unassuming, devoid of all theologizing. *I strictly forbid any of my brothers to interpret the words of the Rule claiming, "This is what they mean." God inspired me to write the Rule plainly and simply, and that is the way you must understand it and live by it, plainly and simply, doing good to the last.* Such a challenge presupposes maturity in faith, as well as humility and detachment from the need to "adjust" Francis' words to fit one's own prejudices. To follow St. Francis implies a willingness to submit to the framework he received from the Lord, the Rule which he had *written down briefly and simply and which his holiness the Pope confirmed.*

The Franciscan Rule is a clean break with a conventional, socially accepted way of life, and at the beginning the brothers experienced it as such: *Those who embraced this life gave to the poor everything they had. They were satisfied with one tunic, patched inside and out, and a cord, and trousers. We refused to have anything more.* It is hard for us today to imagine what the brothers' "break" with their society was like, because today it is by and large respectable to belong to a religious order. Speaking of his own monastic tradition today, Thomas Merton writes:

> With us it is often rather a case of . . . leaving the society of the "world" in order to fit . . . into another kind of society, that of the religious family which [we] enter. [We] exchange the values, concepts and rites of one for those of the other. And since we now have centuries of monasticism behind us, this puts the whole thing in a different light. The social "norms" of a monastic family are also apt to be conventional, and to live by them does not involve a leap into the void—only a radical change of customs and standards.

The same can be said of the Franciscan tradition. The words and stories of St. Francis have in our day become stereotypical fables of the Middle Ages, and they have lost their original shock and challenge. Like the Gospel itself, the way of St. Francis is only known and understood by living it, by making those choices which lead to a radical following of Christ to the cross. Each step of the way involves a dying, a break with conventional wisdom, in order to rise with Christ to a wisdom that transcends mere speculation or learning, a wisdom that comes only from walking in the footsteps of Christ.

How then do we do this in our world? I can only answer by sharing what Franciscan life has become for me. I gave up a long time ago trying to live without money and embraced instead another kind of poverty, the poverty of reputation and respectability that accompanies working with those who are poor in their brokenness and rejection by society. And here I am not necessarily speaking in monetary terms but of that poverty which manifests itself as a sense of failure, or illness, or as emotional or mental disorder that can make one feel more apart and isolated than material poverty might.

Francis of Assisi gave us a way of solidarity with these people, a way of love that leaves us entirely poor in our helplessness and dependence on God. He alone can enable us to love the "unloved" when everyone else is saying we are foolish or stupid to even try, when others are saying such a way can only lead to our own destruction. Life among the "lepers" is always madness to those for whom respectability is holiness and safety is the norm. True poverty of spirit is never in safety but in the risk of looking for God where He said He was to be found, among the least of His brothers and sisters.

Nor is there pride in this choice, because in making such a choice you experience most of the time only helplessness and ineffectiveness as an instrument of healing and wholeness; and God seems so far away, so remote from where He said He would be. And the number of those you can embrace is very limited because of the emotional drain of loving those who are broken; and you are caught up in the dilemma of closeness and distance, problems of what kind of intimacy is proper and what is not, something you do not have to face if you love humanity en masse but never get close enough to become involved with the pain of another.

In Francis I have found a father whose life is a metaphor of everything he believed. The choices he made are, I believe, the choices every person must make in order to become whole, because in every choice he made the primary consideration is always the will of God. Even in great pain and suffering his only concern was God's will: *Once when Francis was very ill, he was so weak that he could not even move. But when one of the brothers asked what he would prefer to bear, this lingering, protracted illness or the suffering of an excruciating martyrdom at the hands of an executioner, he replied, "My son, what has always been and still is most dear to me and sweeter and more acceptable is whatever the Lord my God is most pleased to let happen in me and to me, for my only desire is to be found always conformed and obedient to his will in everything. Yet, if you need to know, this infirmity is harder for me to bear even for three days than any martyrdom. I am not speaking of the reward, of course, but of the intensity of suffering it causes."*

To place God's will above everything else is a further gift of Francis to our world today. We are so concerned with the good opinion of others and with conforming to established ways of doing things that God's will has become fossilized in set patterns of responding to others' needs that can leave the unloved still unloved and God's will a respectable set of rules for remaining uninvolved. I have learned from St. Francis that where there is no involvement with human suffering, there is no following of God's will. And Francis himself learned as much from Jesus, who placed the Father's will above all else: *I came to do the will of Him who sent me.*

Of course, this doing of God's will can itself become a compulsive act, an escape from making decisions, a self-imposed rule as rigidly and blindly adhered to as any set of rules imposed from without. But it was not that way with Francis; doing the will of God was to him what the troubadours called *amour voulu*, a passionate commitment to the love which had begun as a powerful emotion. It was considered unworthy of a true lover to simply be swept away by a fleeting emotion, however powerful it may be. The only response was an exchange of love that was absolute, unconditional, permanent.

This exchange of love is a major theme of the *Sacrum Commercium*, which follows the outlines of the pattern of courtly love that reaches its most profound articulation in *The Divine Comedy* of Dante. What Beatrice is to Dante, Lady Poverty is to Francis in the *Sacrum Commercium*. Apart from this profound exchange of love, Francis' adherence to the will of God is without that unique stamp which characterizes his spirituality. The tradition of courtly love that so captivated Francis as a young boy is the key to the singular viewpoint and flavor that he brought to Christian spirituality. Doing the will of God is not a response to a command to obey but an exchange of love for love, an *amour voulu.*

Just as the courtly lover, the knight of love, undertook painful and often bizarre feats in service to his lady, so Francis' response to the powerful invasion of Love into his life was to carry out daring deeds like a knight-errant proving concretely that he was not the weak victim of an overpowering emotion, but a man passionately committed to Lady Poverty, the unattainable lady of the castle, the spouse of the Lord Jesus Christ. In courtly love the knight's lady was already married to some lord, and the lover was in competition for her love, trying to outdo her lord.

And so it is with Francis. He is in love with the same lady his Lord loves; and because he is infinitely inferior to the Spouse of Lady Poverty, he must do even more dramatic deeds in exchange for so great a love freely given to him. He desires above all else to be conformed to the Lord Jesus, the Spouse and Perfect Lover of the lady whom Francis is trying to woo. That is why Francis seeks martyrdom, the perfect exchange of love. That is why he seeks always the will of God, because it was in response to the will of the Father that God the Word emptied himself of glory and became Jesus, the Poor Savior who embraced Lady Poverty from the beginning of His conception in the womb of a poor Jewish girl and who remained faithful to His lady to the end when He hung naked and totally poor on the Cross.

Without this dimension of courtly love Francis is only a saint among saints; but as the quintessential Romantic lover, he is the personal culmination of that tradition that reaches its highest literary expression in the "Paradise" of Dante's *Divine Comedy* when Beatrice, the poet's lady, herself leads Dante into the sphere of Divine Glory, into the presence of God Himself.

When Dante looks into Beatrice's eyes, he sees reflected there the image of Christ. And that is the vision of Francis of Assisi and why he was who he was: When he looked into the eyes of his Lady Poverty, he saw reflected there the image of Christ. She it is who leads him into Christ, as she had begun very early in Francis' life to be the tangible image of the love of Jesus Christ. As Dante met Beatrice briefly on the streets of Florence and there began one of the great stories of all literature, so Francis met his Lady Poverty in the streets of Assisi, and there began one of the greatest love stories ever lived. As it was written down in *The Legend of The Three Companions*, it goes like this:

Not long after Francis had returned to Assisi, his companions again elected him king of the revels and gave him a free hand to spend what he wanted in preparing his usual sumptuous meal. After the banqueting, they left the house and began singing through the streets. His companions were leading the way, and Francis, holding his wand of office, followed a short distance behind. He wasn't singing, but listening very attentively. Suddenly, the Lord touched his heart, filling it with such overpowering sweetness that he could neither speak nor move. He could only feel and hear this overwhelming sweetness which so completely detached him from all other sensations that, as he later remarked, had he been cut to pieces on the spot, he could not have moved.

When his companions looked around, they saw him in the distance and turned back. What they then saw filled them with amazement: He had been transformed into another man, and they asked him, "What are you thinking about? Why didn't you follow us? You weren't thinking of getting married, were you?"

Francis answered in a clear voice, "Yes! I was thinking of wooing the noblest, richest, and most beautiful bride ever seen." His friends laughed at him and said he was a fool and did not know what he was talking about. Actually, he had been speaking by divine inspiration.

Then the narrator adds these words: *The bride was really that form of true religious living which he embraced.* In Lady Poverty Francis discovers the face of true religion, and in her eyes he sees the image of Christ. That is his gift to us; he taught us how to love this Lady. We need only find her face in our world and, recognizing her beauty, begin again to love her with a passionate, committed love.

17

Evil

We live entangled in distractions of our own making: the pull of the people we make necessary by our need to be loved; responsibilities whose fulfillment satisfies our need to accomplish something worthwhile; the need to please. Always it is our needs which distract us from the one thing necessary, the one thing through which they can be satisfied. The simplification of our lives is not so much in what we rid ourselves of as in what we concentrate on, what focuses the soul.

Francis was so centered on God that nothing was a distraction, and his own needs were forgotten in his absorption in God. How could anything distract when *in every work of the artist he praised the Artist; whatever he found in the things made he referred to the Maker. He rejoiced in all the Lord's handiwork and saw behind things pleasing to the eye their life-giving purpose and cause. Through his footprints impressed upon things, he followed the Loved One everywhere; from all things he made himself a ladder by which he ascended even to his throne.*

But there is more here than the simple response to beauty, more than seeing the footprints of God in creation. It is not just that Francis concentrates on the Other and everything is seen in Him, thereby becoming an aid to contemplation. Something else has happened in Francis to make possible his total concentration on God.

Our greatest distractions come not from the beauty of the world but from the evil in the world and in the self which we have not yet faced, which we try to suppress or deny. The religious person who cannot accept the reality of evil normally sugars everything with piety and distances the self from evil by loving in generalities; loving the poor, all people, nature, creation, etc.

It is hard to picture and therefore to feel a generality like "the poor," or "evil"; and what I don't feel or cannot picture, I don't have to face. And so in moments of true prayer concrete images of this poor woman, this evil tendency in me, that newspaper picture of a murder victim lying in the street rise to the surface of the mind to haunt me and "distract" me from my self-righteous pursuit of generalities.

Francis lives in the concrete world and embraces real lepers and criminals, scandalous priests and ravenous wolves. He embraces his own evil and potential for evil and even carries on a dialogue with the darker side of the self and with the concrete instances of evil that he encounters.

There are two classic stories told of how Francis dealt with evil that stem from a central insight he received from God. It came to him at the beginning of his conversion when he was praying in caves around Assisi. He began to be haunted by the image of a monstrously hunchbacked woman and the fear that he would become like her if he continued on the path of humiliation and penance.

That is, of course, the great fear: that I will become what is most repulsive and terrifying to me, that insanity or physical deformity is somehow contagious and must be avoided at all costs, so that whatever is ugly or disgusting is ostracized, separated by walls or taboos or exile. But then from Francis' depths, he hears the God within: *Francis, what you have loved vainly in the flesh you should now exchange for things of the spirit, taking the bitter for the sweet.*

These words completely change Francis' life, for he had thought, as most beginners in the spiritual life, that God is all sweetness and light. Now he realizes that God is bitter, that he is to choose what is seemingly repulsive instead of what is beautiful; and when he does, as in the incident of embracing the leper (which follows immediately upon the vision of the hunchbacked woman), what is bitter is transformed into sweetness of soul for him, and he recognizes God.

Everything, even evil, is transformed into good by the embrace of divine love; and we do not see things as they are until we take the bold step of overcoming our conventional perceptions of what is attractive and what repulsive by reaching out in love to what is repelling us.

The two stories which complement and illustrate the centrality of this insight in Francis' spirituality are the story of Perfect Joy and the story of the Damietta Prostitute.

Brother Leo asks, Father, I ask you in God's name to tell me where I can find perfect joy.

And St. Francis answers, "Well, my brother, let me tell you a story. We are on a journey. We arrive at St. Mary of the Angels, soaked with rain and shivering with cold, soiled with mud and aching with hunger; and we knock at the gate and brother porter throws open the door and says angrily, 'And who do you think you are?' And we say, 'Why, two of your brothers.' And he laughs at us, saying, 'You're lying. You are a couple of bums who go around deceiving people and stealing what belongs to the poor. Get out of here!' And he refuses to let us in, but makes us stand outside in the cold and rain, shivering and hungry, until nightfall—then, if we put up with all his insults and cutting remarks patiently, without getting upset and complaining, and we admit humbly and charitably that the porter knows who we really are and that God lets him mock us, Oh, Brother Leo, write down this: That is perfect joy!

"And if we keep knocking, and the porter returns and drives us away cursing and beating us like obnoxious fools, saying, 'I told you to get out of here, you filthy thieves—go to an inn! Who do you think you are, anyway? You're certainly not going to eat or sleep here!'—and if we bear this patiently and embrace his insults with joy and love in our hearts, Oh, Brother Leo, write down this: That is perfect joy!

"And if later, suffering intensely from hunger and cold, with night falling, we come back and knock, and shouting, beg to be let in for the love of God, and he grows still angrier and says, 'You guys are really unbelievable! I guess I'll have to give you

what you deserve.' And he come out with a gnarled club, and grabbing us by the cowl, throws us to the ground, rolling us in the mud and clubbing us so brutally that he covers our bodies with wounds—if we endure all these evils and insults and blows with joy and patience, remembering that we must embrace and bear the sufferings of the Blessed Christ patiently for love of Him, Oh, Brother Leo, write down this: That is perfect joy!"

This story reverses our conventional values and offers the world an alternative to retaliation, a plan for survival which may be the only alternative left in a nuclear age. Certainly, it is the only alternative left untried. Fear alone prevents us from believing that perfect joy does in fact lie in enduring *evils and insults and blows with joy and patience, remembering that we must embrace and bear the sufferings of the Blessed Christ patiently for love of Him.* Can it be that this is the reason for so little joy in the world: that we want the other, even Christ, to bear his own suffering, that it is safer to inflict than to bear suffering, that we have placed our faith and hope in having the advantage, the capability of a first strike?

The story of the Damietta Prostitute takes place when Francis is on a crusade in Egypt. He has just left the sultan's court, where he has tried in vain to bring an end to the fighting between Christians and Muslims. He is walking the road alone when up ahead at a curve in the road he spots a modest inn. He is tired and thirsty, and the inn is probably the last one he will come to before night sets in. So Francis walks to the creaking door and pushes his way inside. There are tough-looking men at the tables, and sensuous women are flitting about them like beautiful moths encircling flames.

He walks awkwardly to one of the tables and sits down. With the swiftness of lightning on Mount Subasio and just as unexpectedly, a lovely young lady is at his side, ruffling his hair and pointing to a little door at the back of the inn. Francis smiles gently at the woman, a girl really—she cannot be more than twenty—and takes her small hand. Then rising, he lets her lead him to the back room.

The room is dark but clean and a fire crackles warmly in the fireplace. They stand facing each other in the center of the room, and he looks steadily into the strangely innocent eyes of the girl. She is almost meek in her curious, childlike expectancy. Francis slowly releases her hand and backs away from her. Then he strips himself naked before her, and keeping his eyes riveted on the dumbfounded girl, he lies down upon the burning hearth. He can see the girl wince as his back touches the red-hot stone.

He lies there perfectly still. Then with tenderness of gesture he beckons her to strip and lie down beside him. The girl is terrified. She thinks he must surely be insane, but she does not run away. She only stands there trembling, and their eyes remain transfixed. Then Francis, unharmed by the fire, rises and puts on his tunic while the girl watches in wonder. He goes over to her, takes her face in his hands, and kisses her chastely on the forehead.

The girl, tears streaming from her young, tired eyes, falls at his feet and kisses them. And Francis, too, begins to weep. He lifts her to her feet and leads her to a small stool before the fire and motions her to sit down. Then he sits on the floor at her feet and tells her the story of Jesus.

The story of the Damietta Prostitute is symbolic of Francis' integration of eros and agape, sexual desire and charity. The fire which does not burn him is his own lust, which has been transformed by his selfless love of the woman soliciting him. He does not flee from her like a shocked and pious hypocrite. Instead, he invites her to join him in *his* kind of love, going so far as stripping before her in a symbolic action of total acceptance of his own body and asking her to do the same, a gesture of acceptance and reverence for her used and abused body. And the woman understands—she is converted to Christ.

We gain and find beautiful only that which we accept in reverence and let God redeem; we lose and find ugly what we reject, so that the great sin is what we exclude, what we don't do: "I was hungry and you gave me no food. I was thirsty and you gave me no drink. I was away from home and you gave me no welcome, naked and you gave me no clothing. I was ill and in prison and you did not come to comfort me." (Mt. 25:42–44) It is what we have neglected, what we have failed to do, which is the great distraction from God. The measure of our absorption in God is the measure of what we have been courageous enough to embrace and accept in ourselves and others.

18

Love Song

I

Again in the night   I find you   poor
ragged beggar twisted in the tangle
of my evasions   my flights through dour
pathless people who shine   blinding the angle
of sight that sees in corners the leper's odor
rising smokeless to the whitened sun.   I am done
I say   repeating repentant lies once more.
Always you   Father Francis   I somehow shun
except to mouth and pen your praises   sore
at heart that I have seldom brought you in
where love of God transforms all sin.

II

The shattered music of virtue statics lifeless
in the charged air of desire.   The moon,
the holy moon diffuse through yellow cloud
and I am loud with coughing up the stuff
of selfishness   heaving the battered heart to earth.

III

Wind tearing through the trees   their branches
scraping the dirty sky   shaking seraphs

to the four movements of waywardness,
and you fall from the arms of Christ
into my open arms and I am heavy
with poverty   light with the burden of you.
You of the poor   you are round of smooth,
your weightless floating drawing me
out to Christ who is inside the dying,
my falling down a rising in the soul,
Christ elevating his wounded heart.

19

Providence

If we disregard Providence and think we have to do all the caring for those we love, we will also think we alone must deliver ourselves from evil. Somewhere along the way we have to let go if we are going to be free. That, of course, takes faith, trust that someone else will catch and care for what we have let fall. For what we let go of, we perceive as letting fall, especially if what we relinquish is a person or a relationship. We feel responsible and guilty; we fear our nights will be troubled.

This is a real fear and not to be dismissed by a casual "God will take care of everything I leave behind on my journey to him." It is true that the Kingdom of Heaven suffers violence and we do leave father and mother, brother and sister, to follow the Lord; but if we do not really believe that God does care for those left behind for the Kingdom's sake, then we are tortured inwardly by a false sense of guilt and responsibility.

The key to our self-liberation here is that who and what we leave behind be left only *for the Kingdom's sake* and not for our own. If following the Lord is simply a choice for self-fulfillment and ridding ourselves of difficult commitments, then ours is not a choice for the Lord or His Kingdom but a choice for self at the expense of others. Not that it is always wrong or bad to choose in favor of self, but when that choice is motivated by a desire to rid ourselves of our "leper," then we pass up the real God for a clean, antiseptic God of our imagining. We are passing by the man fallen among thieves; thinking we are going toward the

Lord, we pass him by, abandoned in a ditch by the side of the road.

God cares for everyone and everything we cannot care for because we are trying to follow in the footsteps of Jesus. And, paradoxically, it often happens that when we place our feet in the footprints of Jesus, we bring with us those we thought we were abandoning. "Follow me" reaches beyond and through us to those who love us enough to want to share whatever it is that is freeing us. And we know deep down that God catches what we thought was falling to the ground.

20

Peace and Justice

Why did thousands of people flock to Francis? Why did a life of such poverty and austerity draw people as to some great treasure? Why did giving away possessions bring more joy than acquiring them? Or did it have anything to do with poverty and austerity at all?

The medieval Italian town was a self-contained world. In the piazzas were the churches where God dwelled, and in the central piazza was the municipal hall where the secular authority resided. To be cast outside the city walls by ecclesiastical excommunication or by secular exile was to be excluded not only from society but also from communion with God—like Cain, exiled east of Eden.

Francis' prophetic act was to turn society upside down by moving *voluntarily* outside the walls and proclaiming that God dwells there as well, that the real Kingdom is with the lepers and outcasts who live on the plain below the fortified city of Assisi. God dwells in poor and abandoned wayside chapels like San Damiano, which also lay beyond the city walls and in which Francis heard the voice of Christ from the crucifix.

Francis lives outside the town and draws the people of Assisi there. Beyond the walls there are no classes, and people are no longer victimized and imprisoned by their being either rich or poor; there the provincialism of the local church is absorbed into the Church as catholic and universal where all people are children of the same Father, exiles only from their true home in heaven.

Outside the walls of self and town the Gospel can again be heard and men and women submit once more to the justice of the sermon Jesus preached on the mount outside the walls of Jerusalem:

How blest are the poor in spirit; the reign
of God is theirs.
Blest too are the sorrowing; they shall be
consoled.
Blest are the lowly; they shall inherit the
land.
Blest are they who hunger and thirst for
holiness; they shall have their fill.
Blest are they who show mercy; mercy shall
be theirs.
Blest are the single-hearted, for they shall see
God.
Blest too are the peacemakers; they shall be called
children of God.
Blest are those persecuted for holiness' sake;
the reign of God is theirs.
Blest are you when they insult you and persecute
you and utter every kind of slander against you
because of me.
Be glad and rejoice, for your reward is great
in heaven; they persecuted the prophets before you
in the very same way. (Mt. 5:3–12)

The blueprint for peace and justice is drawn up by Christ himself outside Jerusalem, and Francis and his followers begin to live it anew outside Assisi. The church outside must be repaired if the church inside is to be renewed. What is physical must be rebuilt stone by stone with living stones if the church is to become a living temple of the Spirit.

Only in this way are the barriers between nature and the human city broken down. The garden outside moves inside when the people move outside toward it, when there is no longer inside and outside but a New Jerusalem without walls, and the world becomes a garden again. That is the social message of Francis, a message still little heeded after two thousand years of churches that repeatedly retreat and try to survive inside their own walls.

21

Journey to Rome

My whole life has been filled with journeys and dreams of journeys. The first clear image I have of myself is as a small boy, a plaid, cardboard suitcase in hand, standing manfully on his front porch waiting for someone to take him somewhere. And the second image is like the first—a small boy alone standing along Route 666 trying to thumb a ride to his grandmother's house.

I finally left New Mexico aboard a Cincinnati-bound Greyhound bus when I was fourteen years old. And all my journeys outward and away, even with that first setting forth, were journeys of the soul as well. I remember the way and the places vividly, those outside and inside the mind. And lately, the way itself has become more important, more laced with fire, than arriving anywhere. Perhaps it was always the journey itself that really mattered; perhaps that is one of the ties that secures me to Francis: his journeying, restless soul. Francis seems to be always on the road, always preaching from town to town. And on a deeper, symbolic level his life is a journey to Rome, where he shores up and restores the crumbling walls of Christendom.

After the Lord gave Francis brothers to join him in the following of Christ, he journeyed to Rome, to the court of Pope Innocent III, in order to seek the Pope's approval of his way of life. At that time, before the building of the Vatican, the Basilica of St. John Lateran was the principal church of Christendom and the adjoining palace the residence of the Pope. So it was to St. John Lateran that Francis and his brothers came to request permission and approval to live the Gospel as literally as possible.

Shortly before Francis presented himself to the assembled papal court, the Pope had a dream in which he saw the walls of the Lateran Basilica beginning to fall; and just before they hit the ground, a little beggar caught them and with his own shoulders supported the whole building. And when Francis entered the great audience hall, Innocent III recognized the man of his dream and approved his way of life, because he saw in Francis the one man who could implement the reforms of the Fourth Lateran Council for the renewal of the evangelical life and the restoration of the Church as a spiritual power. And so it came to pass, for Francis became the great champion of orthodoxy and had written down in his Rule that his brothers always remain faithful to the Roman See.

My own struggle with Francis' insistence on obedience to the Roman Pontiff has been with me summer after summer on my way to and from Rome, that city which repels and attracts me simultaneously. And in all those journeys I eventually came to terms with the papacy. I have learned that the men who sit in the chair of Peter affect our lives profoundly as much in who they are as persons as in the doctrinal, moral, and political decisions they make. Those decisions derive from the tradition of the Church and from the Holy Spirit, but they are filtered through men whose background and personality affect considerably both what is said and how it is worded.

In a short span of years we have seen four great Popes strikingly different in temperament and personality: John XXIII, the spontaneous, outgoing peasant; Paul VI, the introverted, careful lawyer; John Paul I, the likable, people-loving journalist; and John Paul II, philosopher, poet, playwright, and significantly, Eastern European Pope. The emphases of these four papacies are as divergent as those of Bergamo, Milan, Venice, and Krakow. Each man is very much a product of his homeland. Each has had a different style and in some cases a different vision of the Church and of the world. Each has been a center of controversy in the Church, a center around whom different viewpoints wage their battles.

My own attitude toward the papacy is one of continuing ambivalence. My faith is grounded in the faith of the Roman Church, but my attitudes are American. The democratic roots of my own homeland are so deep within me that on the emotional level I measure most decisions by how much participation of the people there is in them. I trust the will of the people and feel that God moves in and among them equally with the hierarchy of the Church. My attitude to church is democratic even as I simultaneously put my faith in a hierarchic Church. *There* is the tension. *There* is the source of the ambivalence I feel toward Rome. My attitudes are American, my faith Roman, as Pope John Paul II's attitudes are Eastern European and his faith Roman Catholic.

Seeing these Popes first hand as human beings has helped me to see the Church as human, too. It has helped me to sort out what is human from what is divine. It has made it possible for me to remain American and still be faithful to Francis' promise of "obedience and reverence to his holiness Pope Honorius and his lawfully elected successors and to the Church of Rome."

I know the Pope can speak apart from the people's will and by divine inspiration call them to accountability and responsibility to God. But those occasions are rare. Most of the time God's will is manifest in how people live out their lives. What is universally believed and put into practice is by and large what is infallibly proclaimed by the Vicar of Christ. And in a toss-up between American attitude and Roman faith, faith ultimately wins out for me, because I know my own potential for self-deception and the need for someone apart from myself to act as prophet and call me forth to hear what God is saying. And this conviction is strengthened by what I have seen in my lifetime of whole nations deceiving themselves that something patently evil is OK, or at least should be swept under the rug as if it did not exist.

What the way to Rome has never meant for me is to travel in the national skin of whoever happens to be Pope. A universal acceptance of the nationalism of a given Pope is not what Catholic means. It is one faith, one Lord, one Baptism that makes the

Church Catholic, and we make this journey to Rome, either literally or symbolically, in our own skins, from the particular attitudes that formed us, toward a unity of faith that is not a uniformity of outlook and attitude as well.

22

The Woman of the Desert

Francis, small and bent over like the poor widow of the Gospel, is kneeling before the towering figure of Pope Innocent III, seeking the Pope's permission to preach repentance to the people. The Pope speaks: *My son, go and pray God to reveal whether or not what you are asking really does derive from His most holy will; do this so that we may be sure that if we grant your request we shall be following the will of God.* And while Francis prays, he hears in spirit a parable that reveals the depths of his own soul: *In a desert there lived a poor but beautiful maiden whom a king took as his bride because he was sure she would bear him splendid sons. The marriage contract was drawn up and the marriage consummated, and many sons were born. And when they grew up, their mother said to them: "My children, don't be afraid and timid. Your father is the king. Go now to his court, and he will give you everything you need." When the king saw these children, he marveled at how handsome they were, and recognizing their likeness to himself, he said, "Whose sons are you?" They answered, "We are the children of a poor woman of the desert." And the king joyfully embraced them, saying, "Don't be afraid of anything, for you are my children. And considering how many strangers eat at my table, you who are my lawful sons will do so with far greater right." He embraced them again and decreed that these, his children by the woman of the desert, should be summoned to his court and there provided for.*

Then Francis, rising from the bed of his praying, returns to the Pope and tells him the parable, concluding with this dramatic acceptance of the feminine side of himself: *I am that poor woman and God is the king. In his mercy he has loved and honored me and through me he has begotten legitimate children.*

The Pope is deeply moved by Francis' words and tells him of the dream he himself had had some time before Francis arrived in Rome when he saw the falling basilica saved by resting on Francis' shoulders. The Pope rises and embraces him and approves his Rule and gives Francis and all his brothers the permission to preach repentance to all.

Stunned that his desire has been satisfied so quickly, Francis leaves Rome to begin his life of preaching, but not before a final complementing dream: *He seemed to be walking along a path, and near it there was a great tree, tall, beautiful, strong, and thick. Francis walked up to it and stood beneath it, and he was lifted up until his hand touched the top; and at his touch, the tree gently bent to the ground.*

In mythology the tree is essentially a maternal symbol. And the French Franciscan, Eloi Leclerc, takes that symbol and expands upon it:

> The irresistible pull which emanates from the tree of his dream and draws him to its top, represents a 'return to the mother,' a return for the sake of a new birth, a birth from on high and to a higher life. It is the top of the tree that attracts Francis, and the top of the gigantic tree melts into the heavenly vault; thus it is a symbol of the sacred, of the Most High. . . .
>
> When Francis reaches the top of the tree, he grasps it and effortlessly bends it to the ground. This second movement also has an important symbolical point. In grasping the top of the tree, the hero is in a sense taking the initiative away from the power that has picked him up and raised him to such a height. He thereby affirms his own vocation; he triumphs over the 'mother.' Far from remaining suspended from the tree and entwined in its branches as a bird in its nest is, he goes his own way. . . . He bends it to the

ground, implants it in the earth again. . . . His birth into divine life must be effected through a humble communion with Mother Earth and all the interior, hidden forces she represents.

In Francis' dream there are archetypal echoes of Robert Frost's poem *Birches*.

> I'd like to go by climbing a birch tree,
> And climb black branches up a snow-white trunk
> *Toward* heaven, till the tree could bear no more,
> But dipped its top and set me down again.

The ascent to God, if it is the result of a true birth from the feminine, the maternal dimension within us, is simultaneously a descent into the obscure, dark regions within, so that "the heights of the spirit coincide with the depths of the soul."

In Frost's poem his own weight bends the tree to earth; in Francis' dream, the tree seems to bend of its own accord at the simple touch of Francis' hand. There is a reverence, a delicate gesture implied in that description that is typical of all that Francis does and is, and it symbolizes for me the gentleness of Francis' approach to everything, including his journey to God.

The tree is not his goal, but something he passes along the road which draws him aside and becomes a significant moment on the way to the Father. The tree is an ascending thing that is climbed by descent into the soul. The God who draws our eyes upward to the skies dwells deep down inside our seeing.

23

The Way of St. Francis

Whenever I ask myself why I am a Franciscan or what it is that is unique or special about the way of St. Francis, I always come up with Francis himself. He is what is special. Every Christian spirituality is simply an attempt to take seriously and live more sincerely the Gospel of Jesus Christ, and Franciscan spirituality is no exception. But there is something about Francis himself and the *way* he lives the Gospel that has an irresistible attraction for me. He dares to live the Gospel the *way* I would like to live it, and he loves Jesus the way anyone would like to be loved. He shows how lovable God really is and how much joy loving him can bring.

But there is something more. Francis makes *me* feel loved; he makes me feel that I matter, that I am exciting and interesting and full of potential. That is the power he exercises over us, the Little Poor Man of Assisi, and that is why so many look to him as the model of what they, too, can be. Every person who discovers Francis discovers a friend and brother who somehow understands what it means to be fully human, who understands what life is about, what really matters. Francis is not deceived by the masks I wear; he knows and loves who I really am.

All of this sounds a bit romantic, and it would be precisely that, except for the demands he makes of us. It is impossible to feel a kinship with St. Francis without looking at one's own life and changing something. It is easier to rationalize and dismiss Jesus than Francis, because Jesus, after all, is divine and so far above us. But Francis is only human like us. What he is, we can become. It is the challenge of his life that seduces. We sense that somehow this man found the way, and we are going in the opposite direction. We see in Francis that we are looking for God too high up and too far away. God is inside creation.

Francis realizes and lives out the reconciliation that Jesus Christ has already effected between us and God, us and creation, us and ourselves. His whole life long he tries to choose that reconciliation which is already there in the world around and inside him. Francis becomes one with God through the difficult process of becoming one with himself and all of creation, and he does it the only way he knows how: through following in the footsteps of Jesus and saying yes to everything the Lord has already effected.

And Francis does not set out on his own initiative; the initiative is God's. It is God Himself who leads him among lepers, God Himself who speaks to him through His Word. And Francis goes where God leads, which is where and when we begin to get nervous, to hold back, to rationalize and question.

The tension in our lives derives mainly from holding back the movement of our hearts, from restraining our spontaneous inclination to go all the way and to follow the Lord wherever He leads us. Because we are afraid, we stay with the others who are afraid, while people like Francis move ahead onto that frightening road where they meet all those creatures that we think are our enemies but really are our friends because of the reconciliation accomplished by Christ.

The way of St. Francis is the frightening way of communion with our supposed enemies; it is learning to live again with the lion and the snake that lie in the heart and in the dark woods around us. We are already friends, but we never really know it until, like Francis, we see for ourselves by walking in the footsteps of Jesus. What is so unique about Francis is that he does what we would like to do, and he does it in such a simple, ingenuous way that we know we could do the same if only we would.

24

The Other Side of the Mountain

The way of St. Francis involves a further journey, the explora-
tion of our youth, the other side of the mountain we have
climbed. So if anything further is going to happen in these
pages, I must begin to move backwards to my youth in order to
descend toward the true landscape of the soul. Always it is
movement with Francis, the open road abandoned only to ascend some mountain of prayer.

I return to my roots, to the desert that formed me, the other
side of the mountains that rise above the primeval sand that
dusted my soul as a boy and made the earth an unstable, shifting
thing. I am drawn to the desert like sand in an hourglass up-
turned and counting again. Time is on my mind, soft-sifting,
dragging me through the neck of the glass once more.

I return as I first left, by land to land, the air too dizzy a
height, too fast for arriving without the grief of leaving still
lingering. After flight, which jets ahead of my feelings, I have
not really left. I am still taut with departure.

The distance back must be the way we came away, over the
same ground, the same ache suffered mile by mile, not sped
over at a height that transcends the journey. And so I return
over, but not above, the earth.

The expanse of land between middle age and youth is how far
I have come, how far I must travel to return, each mile an

experience of the heart that in my personal myth is intertwined with the life of St. Francis like counterpoint to a melody.

It was Francis on the road who impelled me at fourteen to leave the desert bound for a future that was somehow a past inside me that had to be claimed, understood, entered into as into a womb. Thus the journey began, and now I retrace my steps with Francis, reflecting on who he is through who he has been for me.

I reach westward to the mountains that watched over my youth. They rise in my imagination not only as the holy mountains of the Navaho, but as the Dionysian counterparts to Mount Subasio that towers above Assisi, that mystical mountain I've scaled for seven summers.

And now as I reach toward the soil of my origins, I realize that the redemptive journey must always be *toward*, even if the destination is the unredeemed soil within. To embrace the other side is to redeem it.

25

The Big Rock Candy Mountain

On a summer's day in the month of May,
A jocker come a-hiking
Down a shady lane in the sugar cane,
A-looking for his liking. . . .

I

When I was a boy and no one else was around, my father would sing to me. We would be speeding along Route 666, invariably toward some fishing hole; and he would sing the same song, as if the fishing trip itself conjured up the images in the old hobo song that lay deep inside his soul. Fishing made the song come true, and every weekend was a trip to the Big Rock Candy Mountain.

Fishing never did that kind of thing for me, but my father's singing did. The song itself came true in the singing, and I would imagine it was all happening before my eyes and that the mountain of the Sleeping Ute that remained steadily on the horizon was really the mountain of the song. We always swerved east just before we arrived at the mountain's base, and the Big Rock Candy Mountain would dissolve and the singing would stop.

Years later when I journeyed to Assisi and stood looking at Mount Subasio towering over the city, the song returned, rising in my mind like a forgotten memory. That was the beginning of my ascending the mountain of the caves where Francis first wrestled his demons and where he preached to the birds and silenced the rushing stream that disturbed his prayer. At the foot of Mount Subasio my father's song rose in my mind, and the way of life I had embraced on a prosaic hill in Cincinnati became the realized fantasy I had imagined life could be.

> As he roamed along, he sang a song
> Of the land of milk and honey,
> Where a bum can stay for many a day
> And he won't need any money. . . .

II

There is something of fairyland in the early Franciscan stories, especially in *The Little Flowers of St. Francis*, which is the most widely read of all the books about St. Francis. In *The Little Flowers* the land of the Big Rock Candy Mountain comes true, but it is not because Francis is an enchanter who casts a spell over the land, nor are the early stories mere fantasies that create a world where our deepest desires can be fulfilled. Rather they are the concrete expression of the return to Eden, the recovery of lost innocence, where people once again commune with the creature world from which they were severed at the Fall. And the way is the way of dispossession. With the primal Fall came appropriation, that clinging to things that hordes and makes one dependent and unfree.

Francis, in his poverty, lets go of all those things we can no longer see or hear because we are holding them too tight. His whole life is intertwined with the difficult process of dispossession, a long journey that leads back to the Garden, where Jesus said "even the demons" would be "subject to us" (Lk. 10:17). "See what I have done; I have given you power to tread on snakes and scorpions and all the forces of the enemy, and nothing shall ever injure you." (Lk. 10:19) And "I solemnly assure you, the one who has faith in me will do the works I do, and greater far than these." (Jn. 14:12)

The stories of St. Francis and the early companions are not just fairy tales; true, they express the fulfillment of those deep desires of the human heart which fairy tales are all about, the world of fantasy where what we really long for comes true. But unlike the world of fantasy, it does not come true simply because we want it to or because we willingly suspend disbelief so that we can enter the world of faerie. The world of St. Francis is the real world transformed only by a conversion from alienation to reconciliation.

Conversion is the beginning of a long journey back through all the stages of our lives from infancy to that stage where we finally turn around to face and be reconciled with what we have denied or fled from in ourselves. The challenge of Franciscan spirituality is to descend into the primitive, primordial darkness of the soul where only God can make light, where all the "enemies" of the soul are redeemed by Jesus, and where the Spirit brings to life the dead bones of one's past.

It is a very personal journey, but as the lives of the early Franciscans show, it can be made only in communion with others who are making the same intensely personal journey. And it is this communion of people together on the road which prevents conversion from being a self-centered affair of the heart, a closed-circuit dialogue between me and the voice I hear inside. Conversion is something that happens in me but also in communion with others.

> Oh, the farmer and his son, they were on the run.
> To the hayfield they were bounding.
> Said the bum to the son, "why don't you come
> To that Big Rock Candy Mountain?". . .

III

What is it that is so difficult about conversion? What is the challenge that is so frightening and that keeps the heart wanting to turn back? Isn't one reason this: that we seem to be regressing? We are going ahead so well, full of plans for the future, ready to reap the rich harvest before us. And then just when we think we are about to arrive, something changes; the hayfield is rotten, and we know that something in us has made it so. We have to start over again. And even if the field of hay is perfect, it disappoints and frustrates our longing, and we don't know why. And so we try to pull our life together and begin anew.

And that is when the trouble really begins. Everything we want to change in ourselves and the road we want to abandon for a new way is so encrusted with habit and attachments, especially those of the heart, that we seem paralyzed. And then the real stickler: Would it be fair to others? How can I go back without those who were my companions on the road, who were my friends? The loneliness of turning my back on those who can't return with me is what keeps me from turning around for long. The promise of a "land of milk and honey" is not enough. Even the refrain of the old song is weak when I think of going back all alone, and the refrain grows fainter in my mind:

Oh, the buzzing of the bees in the cigarette trees,
The soda-water fountain,
The lemonade springs where the blue bird sings
On the Big Rock Candy Mountain. . . .

And then someone like Francis comes along, and there are two of us, and the journey seems more realistic. But still, how can I leave you behind, whoever you are, who have been so much a part of my life? How can I go and not take you with me?

It is the greatness of Francis that he shows us a way to bring with us what we think we are abandoning, what we are separated from. And that is the way of reconciliation.

When Francis renounced his father before the bishop, he was also renouncing his mother; and he experienced personally and painfully, the great rift in creation, the separation between God and people, between people themselves, and the deeper rift at the core of the human heart. There is, as mentioned earlier in these pages, no historical evidence of any reconciliation ever taking place between Francis and his parents; and if in fact it never did take place, the separation must have caused both Francis and his mother and father profound suffering. So it is not surprising that Francis' whole life becomes a response to the reconciliation that has already taken place through Jesus Christ.

Jesus has in fact reconciled all things to God, who is that Fatherhood and Motherhood in which Francis and both Pietro and Lady Pica can share. God becomes the Father and Mother in whom fathers and sons, mothers and daughters find their lost parenthood.

From the moment he embraces God, Francis begins to experience reconciliation with all that before seemed separate from him, including his parents. Francis knows their reconciliation is already effected; and even if there are no human words and acts of reconciliation, Francis knows the truth, the mystery at the center of every human relationship: "It is he [Christ Jesus] who is our peace, and who made the two of us one by breaking down the barrier of hostility that kept us apart, . . . reconciling both of us to God in one body through his cross, which put enmity to death." (Eph. 2:14, 16)

What *we* cannot effect on the human level has already been effected on that same level through the humanity of Christ. We need only to understand and enter into the mystery the plan "to be carried out in the fullness of time: namely, to bring all things in the heavens and on the earth into one under Christ's headship." (Eph. 1:10)

The thorn in Francis' heart was the knowledge that he had not been reconciled with his own parents when he knew they were in truth already reconciled through Christ to their common Parent in Heaven. That we cannot experience humanly what we know to be the underlying truth of a situation is often the deep ache at the heart's core which reminds us that we are not gods but human beings, imperfect, sinful, unable to become or accomplish everything we would like.

The way of reconciliation allows for imperfection and failure, because what we cannot see happening on the surface of life is already accomplished in the hidden depths. Sometimes we have to be satisfied with that deeper reconciliation while we continue to work and pray and hope that what is there already at the core of reality will rise to the surface, and all people and things will become in word and action what they already are: "a dwelling place for God in the Spirit." (Eph. 2:22)

So the very next day they hiked away;
The mile posts they kept counting,
But they never arrived at the lemonade tide
On the Big Rock Candy Mountain. . . .

IV

Three times Francis went off to war, dreams of glory in his mind, and three times his plans are frustrated by God Himself. Each time that Francis left Assisi to join the ranks of some warlord, he was trying to pull his life together, to become someone, to test the limits of his manhood. Ultimately, it was to find meaning by attaching himself to a cause larger than his own concerns, a cause that would free him from the narrow confines of the self. And each time, God frustrates his plans and turns Francis back to Assisi, back upon himself.

From the deep humiliation of returning from battle alone, like a coward, Francis learned one of the most important lessons of his life: The transcendent, the deep meaning of our lives is not in some future battle between armies of horse and armor; the transcendent is revealed in the present moment, in the battle raging within. For Francis the present is not transformed by some future goal, some distant victory, but by surrendering his life to Christ here and now and letting the mystery hidden in the simplest gesture reveal itself.

Francis, by listening to the Lord and returning to Assisi, begins to see the implications of the mystical Body of Christ. In the simple act of restoring, stone by stone, the little chapel of San Damiano, he himself becomes a living stone in "a building which arises on the foundation of the Apostles and prophets, with Christ Jesus himself as the capstone. Through him the whole structure is fitted together and takes shape as a holy temple in the Lord. . . ." (Eph. 2:20–21)

The reason we do not arrive at the "lemonade tide on the Big Rock Candy Mountain" is that we are looking for it somewhere "out there," removed from our present lives, a magical place apart from our ordinary world instead of the magic of the world we already inhabit. The Big Rock Candy Mountain is within our present experience, but only the saint and the poet can see it. For the same reason, so many conversions, so many changes of heart, are short-lived. We are looking for a life "out there," some life in the future different from all the pain and confusion here and now, a life simplified of the seemingly countless entanglements of the present. But a conversion is about my life now. It is a moment and movement of grace that enables me to allow God to transform all the confusion and pain, to simplify my life not by ridding it of conflict, but by enabling me to see and live the mystery hidden at the center of even the most confusing and entangled present.

When I have really surrendered my life to God, everything, even that which seems absurd, is charged with the mystery of His Presence, and I hear and obey His voice arising from the pain and conflict inherent in the human condition. And "the lemonade tide" rises like an artesian well from within my own heart, even when I am doing something so simple as gathering stones to repair some abandoned chapel.

A spirituality which begins with the grand gesture, with the sublime, usually ends with a pile of discarded stones; but one that begins with the simple raw materials of stone and mortar ends with an edifice as solid as the materials that went into it. This truth is at the center of Franciscan spirituality: The design is God's; we have only to listen and provide the menial task of gathering stones and building them firmly one upon another. Though we live often in confusion and full of conflicts within and without, we work for an Architect whose plans do unveil in the present, but only as we continue to work; and only at the end is that plan fully revealed.

The Little Flowers of St. Francis

Mainly they are feet,
these stories, and a tripping
movement light with
what they do not carry.
And the road a trampoline,
shaking dust to the spinning
corners of craziness
gone sane with music.
The little flowers feign
at their feet, careful as
violins between their
brief petals. And you,
Francis, oboe of God,
silly of finger and lip,
somber of breath big
with pressure held back.
The hills are harped
to earth and weather.
The feet pluck the strings
that hold the world together.
See the folk tapping
to your unconscious tunes,
the rhythm of indirection
playing with purpose
a syncopation of water
burning and fire that cools.
The lift and drop of feet
unshod is scoring
the regimented march
into a counter-dance,
a coda of feet in a ring.

26

Social Justice: A Conversation

We sit together in his hogan, the midmorning sunrays falling through the smoke hole onto my lap. And we talk of the spirit and of the Navaho way of reverence for everything that is because it is sacred. I talk of my inability to put into words the spiritual dimension of what we are sharing together. He smiles and says, "Yes, the word that falls on paper seems to stop breathing." And I suddenly realize why so much writing about Navaho myths seems dead on the page.

I look out the window and it is still and hot. Inside, it is cool and silence settles over us. He speaks of the quiet and solitude that is necessary for prayer and for any ceremony of the Navahos. He says, "To understand Navaho ceremony and Navaho ways you must be spiritual. Selfishness and grasping kills the spirit." He speaks of Blessingway:* "In some books about the Blessingway, I read, 'Beauty before me, beauty behind me.' That is wrong. The words should be, 'May the blessing of happiness be before me.' The blessing is what is important because it calls on the supernatural to lead." My reading of Blessingway now begins to clear and I agree.

We talk about the studies that speak of the medicine man controlling evil through his ceremonies. He asks me what I think and I say the studies are probably true. "No, that is wrong. The medicine man is an instrument, like a priest. He performs a ceremony that he hopes will free the person from evil so that

* Blessingway is the most sacred of all Navaho chantways. It is concerned with restoring peace and harmony.

harmony and peace can be restored. Evil is hurting the person, and he must be freed of evil if good is going to dominate once more."

There is a pause and he speaks of classical music. "I like to listen to classical music, because when I do, I experience something spiritual, like a Navaho ceremony." I speak of poetry and he understands what I am trying to say.

The sun through the smoke hole is now flooding my whole body, and we speak of the hogan and of its sacredness. "If you are not spiritual, the hogan is a foolish, inconvenient place to live. If you are spiritual, the hogan is a holy place, the right place for a Navaho to live."

I tell him of my own feeling of wholeness as I speak with him in his hogan, and he smiles. "What is sacred should be spoken in here, because here we are relaxed and comfortable with one another. In the hogan of my father and mother I was prepared for life. One day my father told me that I would someday seek a woman. My father said that the womb of a woman is a sanctuary, for from her comes all of humankind. 'If you stray from the right way, son, you will begin by showing disrespect for woman. If you ever strike your wife, you will know you are already far from the right way.' "

His wife is sitting in the hogan with us, and the gentleness of her face, the quiet of her manner, are proof he heeded his father's words.

I speak of St. Francis and his reverence for people, and he says, "Yes, I know. The first Franciscans out here taught us that by their example. They listened and they learned from us. And we see all the other Franciscans through them. We measure you against what they were and some measure well and some ill."

I am silent, wondering where I stand.

We speak of the Gospel, and he says, "It is like Blessingway. There is no Gospel, no Blessingway without social justice." I am stunned by the use of a formal term like "social justice," and he sees my surprise.

"If you are in need and I hold my corn bundle and pray for you but give you nothing to fill your need, there is no blessing for you or for me. There is no Blessingway if I am selfish with my material goods."

His concept of social justice is so basic and so intimately related to his spiritual life that I can see the two are inseparable. Religion and life for him are one.

I promise to read these words back to him when I have written them down; and I do, and he says that they are right. But he adds, "Remember, these are the thoughts of one man, one Navaho's interpretation." And he shares with me his name, Murray Lincoln, sheepherder.

27

Franciscan Life Today

What is Franciscan living today? The answer is equivalent to asking, What is Gospel living today? And it would be presumptuous of me to answer for anyone but myself. Francis directs me to Jesus and Jesus points to God, the Father and Mother of us all.

It is God as Parent which is revealed when I try even minimally to live that Gospel life which Francis always insisted was the model of his own way of life. When God becomes Parent instead of just Creator, a whole new kind of relationship is involved. Then the whole tension between dependence and independence, between obedience and personal autonomy becomes the ground of my holiness, my wholeness. The same dynamic of love and reverence as for my father and mother, coupled with personal self-determination, is the arena where I work out my salvation. It is a process not unlike the growing, changing relationship with my earthly parents.

In order to follow in the footsteps of Christ, I must leave my father and mother and become a child of God. That does not mean that I am to be childish before God, but childlike, which implies a maturity whereby I have divested myself of masks and become transparently who I am at the core of my being: a child of God, adult in my acceptance of my own contingency, of my own dependence on another for my existence, an Other who is my Divine Father and Mother.

My dependence is ontological, essential, and not a debilitating psychological dependence that expects God to make all my decisions for me. My decisions are my own, but they are possible because of God, upon whom I am dependent for my ability to make those decisions which allow me to grow. Self-determination is rooted in a radical dependence on God, whether I am aware of that dependence or not. And because my dependence is on a god who is Parent, my union with God is the source of and reason for that generativity which fulfills me as a person. St. Gregory of Nyssa writes in one of his sermons: *We are . . . in a certain sense fathers of ourselves when by our good intentions and our own free choice we conceive and give birth to ourselves and bring ourselves to the light. This we do as a result of receiving God into ourselves, when we have been made children of God, children of the power, children of the Most High. On the other hand, we also turn ourselves into an abortion and make ourselves imperfect and sickly when there has not been produced in us, in the Apostle's words, "The form of Christ." For the man or woman of God must be whole and perfect.*

And Francis himself echoes these thoughts in his *Letter to the Faithful*, in which he links dependence on God with obedience as a sign of the interdependence of all creatures upon one another: *We should not want to be in charge of others; we are to be servants and should "be subject to every human creature for God's sake"* (1 Pet. 2:13). *God's spirit will rest on all those who do this and who endure to the end; he will make his dwelling in them and there he will stay. And they will be "children of your Father in heaven"* (Mt. 5:45) *whose work they do. It is they who are the brides, the brothers and sisters and* mothers *of our Lord Jesus Christ. We are his brides when our faithful soul is in union with Jesus Christ through the Holy Spirit; we are his brothers and sisters when we do the will of his Father who is in heaven* (cf. Mt. 12:50), *and we are mothers to him when we enthrone him in our hearts and souls by love, and with a pure and sincere conscience give him birth by doing good.*

My wholeness, my maturity is in my generativity, a fathering and mothering rooted in the Fatherhood and Motherhood of God manifested in the interdependence of all creatures.

I become fully mature when like the Divine Parent I give birth to Jesus Christ, and I can do this only by turning and becoming again a child of God. The child of God gives birth to Jesus. That is the mystery of the Christian life and the heart of the Franciscan way of life: By allowing the father and mother in me to give birth to Jesus Christ in my life, I become my true self.

28

The Way of Dialogue

The way of St. Francis is the way of dialogue. A pattern which emerges from the early sources of Francis' and the brothers' lives is that they spend most of their time in pairs on the road, returning to Assisi once or twice a year for a Chapter of Mats, so-called because the brothers would gather on some hillside and, seated on mats, listen to Francis' words to them. At these chapters the brothers would tell their own stories of what had transpired on the road, confess their sins to one another, and then kneel at Francis' feet as he sent them forth on the road again to preach and witness to the Gospel by their poverty and love for one another.

Francis would say that *when they go about the world, they should not be quarrelsome or take part in verbal disputes* (cf. 2 Tim. 2:14) *or criticize others; but, as people expect of them, they should be gentle, peaceful and unassuming, courteous and humble, speaking respectfully to everyone.* And, *no matter where they are or what situation they find themselves in, all the brothers, like spiritually minded men, should diligently reverence and honor one another without murmuring* (1 Pet. 4:9). *They should let people see that they are happy in God, cheerful and courteous, as is expected of them, and be careful not to look gloomy or depressed like hypocrites.*

Francis' instructions to the brothers were always clear and to the point: They were to witness to the Good News in word and in the way they lived. And that ideal was to be kept before them by sending the brothers forth in pairs in mutual support and witness. The sign to others of the authenticity of their preaching, or its lack, was the way the brothers related to one another.

There is something terribly sobering and leveling in witnessing in community, because it dispels the illusion that we are solitary, single selves and brings a Trinitarian analogue into our witness: two or more persons from whose mutual love the Spirit proceeds. Such relating is not easy, of course, because it constantly curbs our inclination to become gods answerable to no one but God Himself. But human love is in fact the only way to God, because it requires constant dialogue, and dialogue is the very nature of the Trinity itself. To be in dialogue with another is to enter into the very nature of God.

We, however, are not divine, but human, and so we find true dialogue extremely difficult. Honest dialogue gradually exposes the illusions behind which we hide; and because sincere dialogue requires real love and commitment, it also prevents us from isolating our affections in a neat little compartment we reserve for prayer or God or some other safe retreat from the pain of relating, the pain of being one with the communion of saints.

One of the dangers of the so-called spiritual life is the conscious or unconscious isolation of affect. To protect myself from being human I retreat into some "spiritual" life where I need not feel or become involved on the affective level. I spiritualize everything and thereby avoid the messy, complex world where salvation is happening, the world that is groaning and in labor to be born anew in Christ. The isolation of affect makes me neither in nor of the world. And Christ's prayer to the Father is, "I pray thee, not to take them out of the world, but to keep them from the evil one." (Jn. 17:15) And "As thou hast sent me into the world, I have sent them into the world. . . ." (Jn. 17:18)

The model of every Christian is Jesus himself, who though a stranger in the world, was in fact *in* it, allowing himself to be human, to become involved with us; and not just with the saints among us but with sinners and publicans, with the crippled and broken and diseased, even with those possessed by evil spirits. He fed the crowds, he wept over Lazarus his friend, he was wearied by trying to be wholly present to everyone who approached him or called out his name. True religion produces in us the form of Christ, the image of Christ, who was anything but a person who withdrew into the religion of his day to shield himself from the reality of peoples' lives.

Whenever religion becomes institutionalized, it tends to isolate the affections of those who embrace it unless they embrace it as brothers and sisters in true dialogue with one another. And that is why the early Franciscan brothers' and sisters' mutual love and affection was such a powerful sign of God's Kingdom present among us. It made religion credible because of God's Spirit made manifest in that love which is only possible where there is true dialogue, as God Himself is revealed and made tangible in that Blessed Trinity which is a Unity of Persons in dialogue with one another and with us.

29

The Way of Communion

One of the nice-sounding phrases we sometimes bandy about in conversation is "the communion of saints," which capsulizes the reality of our interdependence as human beings transformed into true communion by the common life we share through Baptism. But the faces of the saints are still human faces with all the imperfection of human beings. And the communion among us is continually threatened by the very humanity that bears the divine life which unites us.

Our human relating breaks down because of some sin, or misunderstanding, or hurt; and the whole fabric of our relationships is affected, so that we feel alienated or separated from everyone when it might be our relationship with only one person that is causing the insecurity or loneliness. And because our human relating is tied to our relationship with God, we begin to doubt His love as well when some human love begins to break down. Then it is that "the communion of saints" changes from a nice-sounding phrase to the nitty-gritty reality that it is. Then it is that we are tempted to withdraw and be self-sufficient, to say we don't need anyone, rather than go through the pain of attending to the wound in the Body of Christ.

It is the elevated phrase that can prevent us even from acknowledging that there is a wound in the first place. When we hide behind pious descriptions of human reality, we are shocked when the reality doesn't measure up to the "holy" description of it. "The communion of saints" is really ordinary people trying to live together as human beings who have been baptized into Christ and are thereby profoundly united with one another in him. But the fact remains that we are still ordinary people.

There is a story from sixteenth-century Venice that is an illustration of what I mean. The painter Veronese was summoned before the Holy Office to explain why he had included "profane" matters in a painting of the Last Supper. Why had he included figures of derelicts, passersby, people scratching, repulsively deformed people, someone having a nosebleed, and other such "blasphemous" portrayals in a holy picture? And Veronese simply said, "I thought these things might happen."

It is precisely our naïveté in thinking that some things won't happen among believers that makes for the disillusionment we experience, because we have put a pious binding around a very human reality. For all his simplicity, Francis was anything but naïve about human nature. From the very beginning of his conversion and probably before that, he emerges as a perceptive, realistic man who is not deceived by sham, and he insists again and again that he and his brothers are of the ordinary people and that they be outwardly what they are inside.

Sincerity is all, and we are not to elevate ourselves beyond who we are by pious, eloquent words, or the show of learning, or fine clothes, or precious objects. The early friars were to be who we all are when we are stripped of the trappings of piety or wealth or power: namely, poor, wandering human beings trying to articulate our sorrow and joy, trying to live together as brothers and sisters. And it is the very humanity of the friars which made them so lovable. They wore the clothes of beggars, they mingled with all people, they spoke not in fine phrases but in few and simple words; for, as Francis wrote in his *Rule of 1223*, the brothers *should speak only to the spiritual advantage and good of their listeners, telling them briefly about vice and virtue, punishment and glory, because our Lord himself kept his words short on earth.* Vice *and* virtue; always the balance, always the two sides of who we are.

Nor was Francis naïve about his own humanness and that of his brothers. Neither he nor his brothers were without sin, but they knew the forgiveness of Christ as well, a forgiveness that is made tangible through human beings like ourselves.

In a letter to one of the ministers (the term Francis used for those in authority) Francis makes explicit his profoundly human love for his brothers, even when they have sinned. He writes: *I would like you to prove that you love God and me, his servant and yours, in the following way. There should not be, anywhere in the world, a fallen brother, no matter how far he has fallen into sin, who will ever fail to find your forgiveness for the asking, if he will but look into your eyes. And if he doesn't ask forgiveness, you should ask him if he wants it. And should he come back to you a thousand times, you should love him more than you love me, so that you may draw him to God.*

Only a sincere and human love of who I am behind my masks will ever draw me to God. If being of "the communion of saints" means I can no longer be human and imperfect and sinful, then such a phrase is a pious lie. To say that I belong to "the communion of saints" should define my most profound relating, not be a description of my surface behavior, so that I must walk around, hands folded, *looking* like a "saint."

The surface behavior of the saints is often anything but pious. In fact, the more we are of the saints, the more human we are. If we have learned to love as human beings and to find and experience communion with other human beings, then we are well on the way to union with God. The way of communion with other people *is* the way to union with God.

30

The Way of Mortification

A conversion is a turning around, a change of heart; and mortification is the process of saying good-bye to what is not of God, to what is preventing us from experiencing true peace and joy. The very word is from the Latin word for "death," and implies that we die to those things we mistakenly thought were life-giving and choose what before we thought was death but now realize is truly life. Christian mortification is not self-punishment but embracing the fullness of life.

Today, as in the past, mortification means rejecting those values and patterns of acting that are destroying us; and our conversion, which is even more difficult, means an interiority which will enable us to see through the great lie that some consumer product is the answer to our search for life.

The modern mortification is to start taking care of our health once more out of reverence for who we are: temples of the Spirit of God. Alcohol, drugs, chemicals themselves are destroying in us what they are supposed to preserve. And the new penance is to reject the lie of hype and, following our own common sense, care for that life which has been given us in trust.

That, of course, is no easy task when all we hear and see is that the very things we are rejecting will bring us to life. Instead of prayer time, any respite from hard work or tension is supposed to be pleasure time. When we are bored, we need to reach, not for the challenge of pursuing a life-giving goal, but for an elusive gusto that is prepackaged or prebottled and works its effect immediately.

Our mortification is already cut out for us, and it does not involve punishing the body, or depriving ourselves of food and drink. It involves the dull task of eating and drinking what is healthy and life-giving; it involves the decision to stop killing ourselves and start loving ourselves. And moderation is the key. There is nothing evil as such about alcohol, drugs, sex, tobacco, cosmetics, and luxury travel; but they have all been hyped beyond what they can really do for us, and mere excess has been substituted for what is genuine.

Our whole culture is hyped beyond what it can do and we can tolerate, including our experience of time. Every moment has been accelerated, so that we need the mortification of slowing down and living again the rhythm of nature and our own inner movement instead of trying to keep up with the frenetic pace around us, which most of us have interiorized to such an extent that we cannot relax.

The way of Francis slows us down and leads us into that quiet center within, where God speaks softly the truth of our own worth. It is the way of prudence and charity toward ourselves, as many of the early stories of St. Francis illustrate.

One story in particular stands out in my mind. It takes place at the beginning, when the brothers were living in an animal shed at a place on the plain below Assisi called Rivo Torto. At that time some of the brothers, newly converted to the Lord, were imposing excessive penances on themselves and fasting unreasonably. And it happened that one night one of these brothers cried out, "I am dying, I am dying."

Francis, shaken from his sleep, went to the brother and said, "What is it, brother? *How* are you dying?"

And he answered, "Father Francis, I am dying of hunger?"

Then Francis woke the other brothers and told them to prepare the table. And in order that the brother in question would not be ashamed, Francis began to eat first and invited the starving brother and all the brothers to join him.

And when they had eaten, Francis admonished his brothers that each one should take his own constitution into consideration and not overdo his penances. It was, he said, as great a sin to deprive the body of needed food and drink as it was to overindulge it gluttonously.

This story appears in several of the early Franciscan sources and is always followed or introduced by the narrator's comment that the story is not primarily about food but about Francis' charity and prudence. And so it is, and so, I hope, are these words about mortification: an updating of Francis' prudence and charity for us today.

31

The Way of Freedom

We Americans are supposed to have more personal freedom today than ever. Then why are we often so unfree, so anxious and afraid of life? Why does freedom bring so much insecurity to so many? It has to do, I believe, with a kind of interstellar freedom that is floating in space where relativity has replaced natural laws. We are no longer grounded in our freedom by ties that bind, even by something so fundamental as gravity. It is as if the countless threads that bind us together have been cut, and we are free, but only to experience a free-floating feeling that we are adrift in the universe.

Ours is not the terrifying task of making the choice, even in the face of death, to overthrow an oppressive system which denies us our freedom; ours is the even more terrifying task of making those decisions that will transform a paralyzing license into true freedom. We have the freedom to choose, but we have lost the ground which makes choice possible, that stable center from which self-determination proceeds. The center is still there, but we have lost contact with it through the refusal to become our true selves.

The medieval Franciscan philosopher John Duns Scotus stresses the uniqueness of each individual person which is realized through freedom of choice. I am unique, but I must also choose to become the self that I am. My freedom is in self-liberation, or as the poet Gerard Manley Hopkins would say, in "selving."

> Each mortal thing does one thing and the same:
> Deals out that being indoors each one dwells;
> Selves—goes itself; *myself* it speaks and spells;
> Crying *what I do is me;* for that I came.

Our fear of being ourselves is what is oppressing us, not some totalitarian system, and we are afraid to become ourselves because we have ceased to believe in ourselves; we have settled for a kind of commercial mediocrity whereby we are who we are expected to be by those whose judgment we value, by those who give us the "freedom" to be like everybody else.

The whole Franciscan tradition has been one of reverence for the individual, and nowhere has this position been more penetratingly expressed than in the writings of John Duns Scotus. He preserves the value of the human personality by stressing that the individual and not the species is *being* in the truest sense. And freedom is self-determination rather than the ability to choose one thing rather than another. I cannot, as Robert Frost says, travel both roads "and be one traveler." And yet we try to travel all roads and wonder why we are fragmented. Self-determination involves commitment, and commitment insures my freedom because it is the concrete expression of my selving, of what makes me uniquely who I am.

Francis himself powerfully exemplifies individuality and respect for the individuality of his brothers when on his deathbed he covers the wound in his side as if to preserve the uniqueness of his own way and says, *I have done what is mine to do; may Christ teach you what is yours to do.* And Francis never says we are to *imitate* Christ, but that we are to *follow in the footsteps* of Christ, thus insuring the uniqueness of our own following.

As who we are, we place our feet in Christ's footsteps. Our determination to follow Jesus Christ is a self-determining act that allows Christ himself to shine in a unique way from each individual face. As Gerard Manley Hopkins sings so beautifully,

The just man justices;
Keeps grace: that keeps all his goings graces;
Acts in God's eye what in God's eye he is—
Christ—for Christ plays in ten thousand places,
Lovely in limbs, and lovely in eyes not his
To the Father through the features of men's faces.

For Francis the decision to follow Christ allows him to become who he really is; and when he becomes who he really is, he is free. The ground of all our being is God, and in choosing to follow in the footsteps He left on creation, we rediscover the center from which our personal freedom derives. Only a true self can act freely, and we know that self only in the God who selves through us. In choosing God, we are choosing to be ourselves. God is the tie that binds us to ourselves; Christ is the face behind the masks we wear.

32

Jesus

Everything Francis does or says has its center in Jesus. He embraces himself and others because he has first embraced the Lord, whose love makes it possible for Francis to reach out, even to what is repulsive in himself and others. It is Jesus who shows Francis what it means to overcome shame: *For the divine nature was his from the first; yet he did not think to snatch at equality with God, but made himself nothing, assuming the nature of a slave.* (Phil. 2:6–7) It is Jesus who eats with publicans and sinners, who lives as a carpenter, whose disciples are by and large poor men and women. It is Jesus who has nowhere to lay his head and who dies on a cross, stripped even of the clothing of his self-respect.

It is impossible to overemphasize the centrality of Jesus Christ crucified in the life of St. Francis. This is made abundantly clear in that poignant incident which takes place two years before Francis' death.

With a few chosen disciples he journeys north of Assisi to La Verna, the mountain of his transfiguration, the mountain where he receives the sacred stigmata. There he says the prayer which reveals his intimate relationship with Jesus: *O Lord, I beg of you two graces before I die—to experience personally and in all possible fullness the pains of your bitter Passion, and to feel for you the same love that moved you to sacrifice yourself for us.*

On La Verna St. Francis' search for God ends and his identification with Jesus is confirmed by the wounds in his hands and feet and side. There remains only the sweet embrace of Sister Death which is consummated two years after the stigmata.

Francis lies gravely ill in the bishop's palace in Assisi. At his request the brothers carry him out of the city walls down into the plain where the lepers live and where the little church of St. Mary of the Angels awaits his dying body. He is laid on the chapel's earthen floor and asks that he be stripped of his habit so that he can die naked like Jesus on the Cross. Then to show symbolically the uniqueness of each person's response to God, he puts his hand over the wound in his side.

His song is complete; and when we remove Francis' hand from his side and look into his wound, we see the secret of what it means to love God. We know that our own lives will begin to sing when as individuals and as a world community we, like Francis, let Christ teach us what we are to do. The life of Francis is proof that Christ's words effect union and peace in ourselves and in the world around us if we are brave enough to overcome shame and put them into practice. Words, after all, are illusion until they take on flesh. It is the doing that sings.

33

The Canticle of Brother Sun

I

It was in the spring of 1224 that Francis composed the final poem of his life, *The Canticle of Brother Sun.* "Composed" is perhaps too pretentious a word for this spontaneous outpouring of love and praise that reveals ingenuously the profound unconscious integration that the love of God had effected in his life:

Most high, all-powerful, all good, Lord!
 All praise is yours, all glory, all honour
 And all blessing.

To you alone, Most High, do they belong.
 No mortal lips are worthy
 To pronounce your name.

All praise be yours, my Lord, through all that you have
 made,
 And first my lord Brother Sun,
 Who brings the day; and light you give to us through
 him.

How beautiful is he, how radiant in all his splendour!
 Of you, Most High, he bears the likeness.

All praise be yours, my Lord, through Sister Moon and
 Stars;
 In the heavens you have made them, bright
 And precious and fair.

*All praise be yours, my Lord, through Brothers Wind and
   Air,
And fair and stormy, all the weather's moods,
By which you cherish all that you have made.*

*All praise be yours, my Lord, through Sister Water,
So useful, lowly, precious and pure.*

*All praise be yours, my Lord, through Brother Fire,
Through whom you brighten up the night.
How beautiful he is, how gay! Full of power and
   strength.*

*All praise be yours, my Lord, through Sister Earth, our
   mother,
Who feeds us in her sovereignty and produces
Various fruits and colored flowers and herbs.*

*All praise be yours, my Lord, through those who grant
   pardon
For love of you; through those who endure
Sickness and trial.*

*Happy those who endure in peace,
By you, Most High, they will be crowned.*

*All praise be yours, my Lord, through Sister Death,
From whose embrace no mortal can escape.*

*Woe to those who die in mortal sin!
Happy those She finds doing your will!
The second death can do no harm to them.*

*Praise and bless my Lord, and give him thanks,
And serve him with great humility.*

At every critical moment of his life Francis had broken forth
in song like the troubadours he listened to and admired as a boy.
And in one sense *The Canticle of Brother Sun* is more a song
than a well-crafted poem; it is the swan song of one of the
greatest troubadours of the Middle Ages.

Like the life of Francis himself, this canticle is not a self-conscious work of art. It looks wholly to the Other with the eyes of praise and adoration, and that Other is God revealed in all his creatures. It is a summary of a soul open to everything around it and everything deep within. From the first words—*Most High, all powerful, all good, Lord,*—the canticle hurls the reader upward and outward away from self-centering and that heightened self-awareness which is so highly valued among moderns. It focuses instead on creatures and praises God through them; it is the song of a soul who has lived the truth that only two things really matter: the love of God and the love of His creation.

The Canticle of Brother Sun is a sublime articulation of the secret of Francis' life: you integrate the depths of the self by leaving self and entering into what you can see and hear and touch and feel and smell. God dwells "deep down things," and you find Him when He finds you loving the world He has created and redeemed.

The life of Francis is the story of how one man found God, and the final poem of his life reveals what happened to that man for whom the love of God was everything. And the surprise is that when God is everything, then everything else becomes more important and more holy. The whole creature world is enhanced instead of being neglected and de-emphasized for some spirit world, as so often happens in pseudospirituality. For Francis, whatever demeans and devalues the creature demeans the Creator, so that reverence for and joy over every thing and every person becomes *the* sign of the love of God.

However, this joy of Francis is not the popular notion of the great lover of birds who adorns bird baths all over the world. The circumstances in which Francis sang his great canticle should dispel forever the sentimental picture of Francis of Assisi as a happy "Romantic" skipping through the woods, talking to animals, with a cute little bird on his shoulder. On the contrary, Francis was a man who took quite literally Christ's words, *If anyone would be my disciple, let him take up his cross daily and follow me.* (Mt. 16:24) As Francis wrote for his brothers, *the rule and life of the brothers is following the footsteps of our Lord Jesus Christ.* Where those footsteps led Francis himself is dramatically drawn in the scene of his composing *The Canticle of Brother Sun.*

He has just returned from La Verna, where he has been imprinted with the wounds of Christ. He is suffering what is probably tuberculosis and from a painful trachoma that causes his eyes to bleed and makes any light unbearable. He cannot endure the light of the sun or even a candle by night, so he lives for over fifty days and nights in a darkened hut beside his beloved church of San Damiano. Field mice run back and forth across his weakened body which hemorrhages from time to time from the wounds of Christ which Francis bears in his body. He is in a deep depression over the betrayal of his ideals by those brothers who are becoming more like monks than poor, wandering mendicants. He feels, in his weakened condition, that God has abandoned him, that he is a lost soul, cut off from the love of God by his own sins.

It is out of this terrible darkness that the *Canticle* breaks forth from Francis' soul. No sugary piety here, no ecstatic response to a rainbow, but a celebration of what he himself can only dimly feel in his brokenness, a poem of faith, hope, and love:

> All praise be yours, my Lord, through all that you
>   have made,
>   And first my lord Brother Sun,
>   Who brings the day; and light you give to us
>   through him.
> How beautiful is he, how radiant in all his splendour!
>   Of you, Most High, he bears the likeness.
>   . . .
> All praise be yours, my Lord, through Brother Fire,
>   Through whom you brighten up the night.
>   How beautiful is he, how gay! Full of power and
>   strength.

Only a saint can sing like that in circumstances so different from the words of his poem. Only a man drawing on his past and looking to the future can sing:

All praise be yours, my Lord, through Sister Death,
From whose embrace no mortal can escape.

Francis adds this stanza shortly before he dies, and it reveals his profound acceptance of death, which cannot have happened suddenly at the moment of death. He has embraced Sister Death long before he expresses that acceptance in words.

In a way, St. Francis came into life embracing death. He was about twenty-two years old when he was reborn into Christ, and that experience followed the illness during which he had wrestled with death for a year. He had been taken prisoner two years before in the battle with Perugia. For a year he poured himself out, cheering his fellow prisoners, seemingly unaffected by his imprisonment. When taunted by some of the prisoners for befriending an incorrigibly bitter and sarcastic fellow prisoner, Francis said, *The day is coming when the whole world will honor me.* Little did he realize then the price he would pay for that honor.

For when the brash, enthusiastic young Francis was finally released from prison and returned to Assisi, he fell into that deep illness which confined him to his bed for over a year.

And now two years before his death he is again wrestling with death, and once again in embracing her he rises to new life in God. There is a further peace, a deeper union with God during these last two years, and Francis no longer seems anxious about the Order he has founded.

The reason for his optimism is his own personal peace. He knows through a vision that takes place shortly before he sings his canticle that he will be with Jesus in Paradise. He is assured of blessedness. Throughout his life Francis' cosmic optimism derives from his personal peace of soul; if all is well within, all is well without. When we are secure in our primary relationships, then the world around us is safe. But if our most important relationship is threatened, then the world is unsafe; we begin to fear death because of the emotional death that is threatening us.

II

All praise be yours, my Lord, through Sister Death,
From whose embrace no mortal can escape.

He urged even death to give praise, and going joyfully to
meet it, he invited it to take up lodging with him. "Wel-
come," he said, "my sister death."

As a boy, I used to think how wonderful it would be to have
the kind of faith present in these lines of Francis. I used to think
it would be so consoling and uplifting to be a saint and know
that death was nothing to be afraid of because God had revealed
himself to you and you were eager to be with him forever in
heaven. Then one day years later, while I was anxiously thinking about my own death, I heard Francis' words, "Welcome,
Sister Death," and made them my own, and everything
changed. I experienced a profound peace and I understood
what had happened to Francis.

It is not that God came to him and therefore he was not afraid
of death. Rather he embraced death as if it were life itself, and
then God came to him. The frantic activity of our lives is often
only our futile endeavor to escape death, an effort which is itself
death-dealing. To say yes to death is to embrace life. To accept
death in anticipation of life, as Francis did, is to become wholly
alive and free. And to praise God through death and embrace
her as a sister enables one to welcome her when she comes.

If what I have just said is true, then Francis is one of us. He can
no longer be used, as the saints often are, to prevent us from
dealing humanly and realistically with our own deaths. He had
to struggle like we do before he could have said so astonishing a
thing as "Welcome, Sister Death." Not "Welcome, God," or
"Welcome, eternity," but, "Welcome, Sister Death." No one
could utter those words without first having suffered a kind of
martyrdom of mind and heart that leads to one's own resurrection. As Francis himself once wrote, *We ought to be ashamed of*
ourselves; the saints endured the agony of the cross, but we who

call ourselves servants of God try to win honor and glory by merely recounting and revealing what they have done.

There is no substitute for experience, no vicarious holiness. It is clear from Francis' life that the saint acts upon God's word. We, on the other hand, are always waiting for God to make himself present to us before we are willing to act. The saint experiences the resurrection while he or she is still living on earth, not because God reveals it, but because the saint has already passed through the fear of death by actively embracing life-giving death and inviting *it to take up lodging with him.*

As the poet Rainer Maria Rilke has written so poignantly:

Be ahead of all parting, as though it already were
behind you, like the winter that has just gone by.
For among these winters there is one so endlessly winter
that only by wintering through it will your heart survive.

III

St. John of the Cross says in one of his writings that the Resurrection is interior to the Cross. I take that to mean that our rising takes place in the midst of our suffering. It is not that we go through suffering waiting for the resurrection to happen in our lives; rather we experience the Resurrection of Jesus right in the center of our pain and suffering. That is why the saints could rejoice in their sufferings which united them to Christ and thereby to His Cross, which is always joined to His Resurrection. Our suffering is redeemed by the Resurrection of Jesus, whose own suffering and death carried the seeds of the Resurrection inside them.

Everyone who has surrendered his or her sufferings to Christ, knows that in that surrender there is already a peace that begins to root in the heart like a seed that we know will flower. Before surrendering, we are anxious and afraid and full of anger. We wonder why God is permitting this to happen to us. We are bitter and unhappy. Because we refuse to let go, we cannot experience the resurrection that is already beginning in our suffering. But once we surrender like Mary and say in effect,

"Let it be done to me according to your will," our very suffering begins to seem like a rising to God.

The resurrection of the soul presumes a dying that is an acceptance of whatever the Lord is asking us to let go of, and sometimes what we cannot let go of is our own suffering. We want it to end, so we can rise. We want God to make everything right and good again so that we can get on with our lives. But God might be asking us to embrace our suffering and confusion and pain that *He* might begin to shine in our lives. And what we might have to get on with is a life very different from what we expected, a new life that rises constantly despite its pain and confusion and suffering, because it is a life of surrender to His will who alone can make rise what seems to be bound to earth.

This acceptance of God's will is why St. Francis could sing a song of joy like *The Canticle of Brother Sun* in the midst of extreme pain and suffering. He was able to let go and give his suffering to God, because he saw in a vision that all of this misery was as nothing compared to the treasure buried inside it. And at that moment he began to rise; at that very moment when he was most like Jesus on the Cross, he began to rise. He lifted himself from the cot of pain on which he lay and sang *The Canticle of Brother Sun,* which was and is the Easter song of every Franciscan heart.

IV

Sometimes when I am reading *The Canticle of Brother Sun,* I get the strange feeling that Francis is in the poem looking out at me. I sense his eyes on me from inside the creatures through which he is praising God. He is inside the sun feeling what it is like to be God's instrument of day, to be beautiful and radiant with light. How deeply Francis must have contemplated the elements of his canticle that he can inhabit them so intimately, that he can only talk about them from inside their being. So profoundly does Francis' canticle move me that I cannot look at moon and stars without seeing Francis' eye upon me, shining from within them, proclaiming them "bright, and precious and fair." Only it is *he* who has become "bright, and precious and fair" inside them and they in him.

He is inside Brothers Wind and Air moodily eyeing me from "fair and stormy, all the weather's moods," which are somehow God's moods as well, and I hear Francis' voice inside the wind startling me with the truth that God cherishes all he has made through *all* the weather's moods. To what depth of weather must you descend to recognize a devastating storm as God's *cherishing* his creatures?

And in Sister Water I glimpse Francis finned, returning to his primal origins moving in water that has become "useful, lowly, precious and pure." On a summer's day I sometimes see Francis playfully breaking through to the surface of a pond from some deep underwater fathoming where he has wed the feminine side of who he is and grown comfortable enough to swim through and in her, breaking surface from time to time to speak to us from inside water.

In Brother Fire I see not only Francis' eye but his whole body feeling "beautiful and jocund, robust and strong," and I hear him singing that the flames which illumine the night do not burn us, and they illumine our whole being if we can somehow get inside them and look from them on all that is not on fire.

And I can feel Francis' spirit pushing up through Sister Earth in "various fruits with colored flowers and herbs." He somehow becomes their inner movement in the way he seems to emerge from the earth whenever he lifts his arms in praise. Francis is his poem; or better still, his poem is who he has become.

34

Francis: A Personal Reflection

The sky is blue this morning with only a hint of cloud on the horizon. The trees in the woods beneath my window are green with that light, first green of spring. I am alone here, but I don't feel alone, because I belong to this paper and pencil, to this desk and the view through the window, and to everyone who is not here with me.

Always when I reflect on the meaning of St. Francis in my own life, I arrive here at this point of myself in communion with everything that is. The gift of trying to live the way of life he gave me, even in my many failures to live it well, has been the experience of interconnectedness, the shattering of the shell of loneliness and despair, that illusion which surrounds and contains the isolated self.

We live in a time of loneliness, a paranoiac age that encircles nations of isolated individuals with defenses that cannot defend and that invests human intimacy with a magical power it does not have. I am part of this world, and I am constantly tempted to believe that bombs and one-to-one intimate love can make me secure. But when I give in, even for an instant, I hear an echo of something Francis said, or a scene from his life flickers faintly in my mind; and I am reminded again of the vision he gave me as a boy which has proven over and over again to be true.

That vision is simply this: The exclusive love of anyone or anything is essentially isolation and leads to loneliness. Only a love that is inclusive of everything God has made can make me whole, and to the extent that I can belong to the universe without trying to cling possessively to anything in it, to that extent am I freed of loneliness.

However, it is not enough to know this great truth intellectually. I must live it out as Francis did. And that means a constant dialogue between myself and God, myself and people, myself and the things of my experience. True communion implies dialogue, and that is what I see in Francis' speaking and listening to birds and other creatures. That is what I see in Francis' living among the lepers and dressing their wounds and listening to their stories. Only in communion that leads to dialogue are the great paradoxes of the spiritual life made real: poverty that is wealth, suffering that is joy, bitterness turned to sweetness, crucifixion turning into resurrection from the dead.

When there is no articulation of joy and sorrow, the self remains imprisoned and begins to protect itself from that which can save it: the Other.

Each morning as I read the newspaper, I see paragraph after paragraph of talks, negotiations, and treaties made and broken; but seldom is there any real dialogue, because neither side (and to say "side" is already to negate dialogue) articulates its real fear, risks saying what it is that really divides and separates people and lands: the fear of poverty, suffering, crucifixion. In short, it is the fear of powerlessness, dependence, loss of control that widens every negotiating table, making impossible any reaching across to join hands.

The vision Francis gave us was the truth of our essential poverty vis-à-vis the Creator. Before him we are all powerless and dependent. We are all his creatures, and he is Father/ Mother of us all. What that means practically is that until we embrace our fundamental creaturehood and know experientially that we are not gods, we cannot know our essential communion; and instead, we try to best others, to come out on top, to control people and even nations of people to prove our own "omnipotence."

In other words, in Francis I see someone who knew who he was in God, and therefore he knew who everyone else was as well. For him every human dialogue has as its reference point the God whose Word is inside every true word. Francis trusted in that truth when he marched boldly into the camp of the sultan in Damietta. He knew if he entered into true dialogue and spoke the truth, the sultan would recognize the same God in Francis' word as in his own, and he would recognize that they were brothers.

Francis emerges as authentically human because by listening to God's Word, he knew who he was, and others recognized their true selves in him, the selves they were denying out of fear. The poverty and suffering Francis embraced is the poverty and suffering of the human heart externalized. He brought outdoors what lies deep inside even the most seemingly self-assured, self-sufficient human being.

What Francis showed us all is that self-sufficiency is an illusion. We all need one another and we need God in order to know that we do need one another. And once we embrace our basic dependence on God and interdependence on one another, once we face and articulate the deep fear that keeps us from acknowledging any kind of dependence, then true dialogue is possible, that freeing dialogue that gives us the independence we were so afraid of losing.

Francis' model of human liberation is Trinitarian. The God of the Old Testament is One in splendid isolation from his creation until the Word he utters from all eternity is revealed to us in Jesus, and we know a Trinity of Persons, the model of our own human loving. Not in twos but in threes does communication become communion. And the third Person, often missing in dialogue, is God Himself, the God I deny when I refuse to let go of my own need to control, when I refuse the power available to me only in powerlessness.

I am sure that to many this seems the most naïve, even "pious," kind of theorizing. But is it? Don't we often project the darkness and fear of our own hearts onto those around us? Aren't there times when because we are afraid to acknowledge something dark, even to ourselves, we find it in others instead and reject them because they remind us of something we have failed to come to terms with in ourselves?

Whenever Francis is seemingly denigrating himself and insisting on his own worthlessness and unworthiness, I like to think he is simply acknowledging his own human imperfection, his own potential for evil, so that he won't start seeing in others what is really in his own heart. The dialogue he carries on with creatures is an extension of the dialogue he maintains with himself. And because he is brave enough to face and communicate with his own self, good and evil, whole and fragmented, he is able to risk dialogue with the imperfect creature world around him. And because it is a dialogue in God, that third redeeming Person, a profound reconciliation takes place at the heart of his communing with self and nature.

From this modeling that Francis left me, I have come to see the whole business of living as a process of inner and outer reconciliation that begins when I forgive in myself what I previously thought was something coming from without, some evil pressing in from the universe outside me. What we see around us is also inside our own hearts, at least potentially. And to the extent we can forgive ourselves, to that extent only can we forgive and be reconciled with our world.

Francis, then, is more than some nature mystic; he is a mystic of the soul who communes with God through nature as a mirror of his own soul. And this approach has enormous implications for us today. For if the world around us is a reflection of who we are as individuals and as a people, then world peace and reconciliation with the whole creature world begins with personal peace and inner reconciliation.

We need to find and embrace the God who dwells inside the darkness of our hearts, beckoning us to make the frightening journey through the darkness to the light at the center which we cannot see unless we travel through and become reconciled with our own personal potential for evil. An honest look at ourselves will reveal what needs to be done to transform the world around us: It is simply to respond to the age-old call of God to every person and all persons to change their hearts by accepting the gift of a new heart from Him. That is the response that Francis made, and it is the genuineness of that response which has made him the supreme model of the peacemakers we are all intended to be.

35

The Journey Inward

Who could feel sorry for St. Francis because he threw away his clothes and took the vow of poverty? He was the first man on record, I imagine, who asked for stones instead of bread. Living on the refuse which others threw away he acquired the strength to accomplish miracles, to inspire joy such as few men have given the world, and, by no means the least of his powers, to write the most sublime and simple, the most eloquent hymn of thanksgiving that we have in all literature, "The Canticle of the Sun." Let go and let be! . . . Being is burning, in the truest sense, and if there is to be any peace it will come about through being, not having.

HENRY MILLER

The hardest way of all is the journey inward. It is a journey which cannot be made without letting go of those supports which keep us from relying wholly on God. It is, in Henry Miller's words, a "burning, in the truest sense," a burning up of what is superfluous outside us because of the consuming fire within.

The truly interior person stands burning at the center of the universe; and unless we suffer this fire within, everything we are trying to preserve will be consumed by that fire created from the rejected burning of countless hearts that splits the atom at the heart of all being. If we refuse to burn, to suffer for one another, our collective guilt will make us enemies, and we will end up destroying one another to rid ourselves of the evil which really lies within and can only be transformed by fire.

The fire from the sky or the fire that burns within; never has the choice been so clear. It was always so in the affairs of humankind, but now that we have it in our power to destroy the very planet upon which we have always found some place to escape, we are forced to turn inward to escape the conflagration we thought would deliver us from evil.

And so we begin at the end of the second millennium the journey into the heart, a journey that is both a burning and a burning up, a journey Jesus himself invited us to make at the beginning of the first millennium and St. Francis reminded us was still valid at the beginning of the second millennium. And now the Bomb itself has become the ultimate, uncompromising herald, announcing that we all have to make the journey inward or perish from the extremes that our journey away from ourselves has produced.

Our flight from the fire within into the security of matter has metamorphosed matter into a destructive energy we thought we were escaping. Matter itself contains in its core the fire that only inner reconciliation can transform into love rather than hate. The Bomb derives from the same fire that makes a grain of wheat grow. Wheat is slow and organic and reverent like love; the Bomb is mechanical and swift and willful like hate. Wheat grows when we let it go and let it be. When we force it, it eventually explodes.

To let anything go and let it be is not easy. It always causes a slow, smokeless burning in the human heart. But that burning is really what it means to be. And if we do not make the journey inward to see for ourselves that to be is to burn and that burning is active and passive simultaneously, then we will try to distract ourselves from inner fire by an outer fire that loads matter with explosives to burn up the potential fire coming at us from the "enemy."

The journey inward is the only journey that will enable us to survive. For at the center of the journey is the Bomb we thought was going to fall from the sky. It is ticking within us and can only be defused by a personal and collective journey into the heart.

Only there at the core can we choose between the fire of love and the fire of hate, because only there are we truly free of fear. We overcome fear on the journey inward to the heart or we never reach the center of the heart at all. We travel in fear into the fire which consumes the fear we carry with us into the flame.

And it all begins when we ask for stones instead of bread, when we start to restore what is falling into ruin, to shore up and strengthen and build instead of worrying about what we are to eat. From the time of the Garden of Eden till now *the* temptation is to ask for the bread we cannot have instead of celebrating the Creator through the bread he has generously given.

The journey inward is a journey that enables us, in the words of the American Catholic bishops, to "read the Book of Genesis with a new awareness; the moral issue at stake in nuclear war involves the meaning of sin in its most graphic dimensions. Every sinful act is a confrontation of the creature and Creator. Today the destructive potential of the nuclear powers threatens the sovereignty of God over the world he has brought into being. We could destroy his work."

Those are the two fires: Creator and creature. In usurping God's role in creation, we will destroy ourselves, for we seek to preserve with a destructive fire that is out of control because it is totally under our control. The redeeming Fire is within; God is within where we banished him when we took upon ourselves the sovereignty of the universe.

God will not be released in the transformation of matter into energy but, as St. Francis saw, only in "the transubstantiation of matter into spirit," a process that takes place at the center of the human heart. And it all begins with stones that become a living temple upon whose altar bread and wine are changed into Food which transforms the heart so that it prefers a burning that is being to a burning which is having, the sound of a canticle of thanksgiving to the sound of the atom rudely torn asunder. And the sun, not the Bomb, becomes the symbol of the Sovereign Fire of the universe.

*All praise be yours, my Lord through all that you have
    made,
And first my Lord Brother Sun,
Who brings the day; and light you give to us through
    him.*

*How beautiful is he, how radiant in all his splendour!
Of you, Most High, he bears the likeness.*

Afterword

All the way to heaven is heaven.

CATHERINE OF SIENA

I try once more to express what it is about Francis that is still so attractive to me as I approach my middle years. It does not focus on the Francis of my youth or young manhood: The Little Poor Man who leaves his father's house to restore the house of God, or the Herald of the Great King who walks the roads of the world proclaiming the Gospel of Jesus Christ more by example than by word, the "martyr" who walks boldly into the camp of the sultan in Damietta to preach repentance and to witness to Jesus.

That young Francis still attracts me, but not so much as the Francis more my own age who sees the high romance of the beginnings of his dream fade away and his ideals eroded by the compromises of his brothers, who sees his health deteriorating and Sister Death approaching his hut on the plain below Assisi.

His face is without masks, but it is not without pain. Earth, water, air, and fire have left their traces in the furrows of his brow, in the sweat upon his beard, in his tousled hair, and in the blood of his eyes. His is the face of the primitive, of one who has plunged headlong into the creature world as into and through the mirror of his own psyche. And once through the looking glass, he learns to reconcile the opposing faces within himself and within all of creation.

He learns to embrace the elements of the universe as his

brothers and sisters: *Brother* Wind and *Sister* Water, *Brother* Fire and *Sister* Earth. He learns it all through lepers, the first persons he recognizes inside the glass.

What draws me close to this Francis in his early forties is his altogether sacramental vision of reality. Perhaps it is because only that kind of vision redeems my own life now and transforms the routine of daily living, the monotony of what we call being alive. Only a sacramental view can keep us from despair in a nuclear age, or any age.

It is hard to say just what this sacramental vision is, except that it is not the Big Rock Candy Mountain of my dreams so much as it is the attitude of the bum in the song who seems to create the Big Rock Candy Mountain wherever he goes. The bum himself says to my heart that the Big Rock Candy Mountain is not just the destination, but the way there as well.

Only the sacramental vision can make a heaven of the getting there, a vision which sees everything as it really is: a sign of the presence of God. The sacramental is what integrates our going to God with our arrival. And unless we so unify our lives that there is a heaven in the way to heaven, then there is a split, a kind of schizophrenia between our day-to-day living and our so-called spiritual life.

If I am always doing things in order to get to heaven, I have not embraced my getting there as lovingly as I have embraced my final destination.

The image that comes to my mind here is that of an early-morning jogger. If I get up in the morning to jog in order to keep physically fit, but don't really love the sometimes ecstatic rhythm and feeling of movement with the universe, then my exercise is out of harmony with my living. Then if on top of this disharmony the rest of my day is crammed with strain and activity which is harmful to my health, I am pushing physical fitness into a separate compartment of my life and not really carrying the natural rhythm of running throughout my entire day.

I like the image of jogging because it relates so directly to the body, which is where I believe a sacramental spirituality begins. Unless I am comfortable with my own body and love it, my striving for wholeness, or union with God, (which is what spirituality is all about) easily becomes an escape from the body, an unnatural splitting of body and spirit. If I can only become spiritual, then that dirty old body will somehow go away!

How far from true Christlikeness that attitude is. Jesus, the Son of God, becomes human, redeems us in and through his body, rises from the tomb and appears in a glorified body only to see some of his followers striving to become "spiritual" by rejecting the bodily dimension of their lives! I am a whole person, and until I love my body as much as my soul, I will not be a truly complete human being. My body is a sacrament of the presence of God.

I understand all of spirituality as the slow work of God's grace bringing together body and soul in each of us. When the two merge in our consciousness as they do in reality, and we embrace that merging and love it, then we are on the way; and our going to heaven is as beautiful as our arriving there.

The great work of integration is God's work, but it is slow because of our prejudices, our hang-ups about ourselves. We find it difficult to love ourselves because of years of acquired self-hatred that affects the way we view ourselves through our outward image, the body. And seeing the body as an outer image of an inner self is already a division. I am my body; and therefore I must embrace my body if I am going to embrace myself, simply because body and soul are one person.

A professor of theology once asked his class to write an essay on salvation, and one of the students handed in a "perfect" paper. On both the front and back of one sheet of paper, he drew the same picture of himself standing in front of a mirror. The caption at the bottom of the front side read, "God loves you." On the reverse side was the caption, "I love you." A six-word essay that in its brevity says everything! I look at myself in the mirror, and I hear God saying, "I love what you see." I look again, and I am able to say, "I love what I see."

What is it that makes it so difficult to accept and celebrate this whole person I see in the mirror? I hope I am not oversimplifying, but I believe it is evil. Evil divides; grace integrates. I am born into a world in which evil is a given reality. It is there and so is the division it brings—division between God and the human person, between one human being and another, between body and soul. And all of God's working in the world is a healing of that division, a bringing together, a reconciling that is moving slowly toward unity.

It is easier to see the division, the evil, in our lives than it is to see God's loving hand working toward our eventual coming together in Him. Perhaps an example of what I mean is a person dying of a terminal disease, certainly a dramatic instance of evil, of that seeming division of body and soul. I can begin to hate my body as my enemy because of what is happening to it, or I can embrace its suffering, its dying, as the beginning of my final integration. The way people react to death is the way they have reacted to life, to those moments of living which have often included a little dying, a little letting go that worked a further wholeness, a further loving.

True religion is loving God with my whole soul and my whole mind and my whole body as a whole person. Soul, mind, and body are a "minitrinity," that is, a unity, one person. It is only when I am one that I can love others properly, because I love them as myself. If my self is divided, so will be my love of others. If I love my soul and hate my body, then when I love you and embrace you, you will not feel loved at all. I am loving something unreal, a disembodied soul inside of you that is good, that is godlike in spite of your "bad" body. There is no such thing. If I truly love you, I love you, whole and entire, just as you are.

Someone once said, "Holiness is wholeness." And so it is. No one is ever perfectly whole, but working with God toward wholeness is the grand adventure of life. It is spending your life on the right thing; it is the direction in which all your energy should be channeled, and it is achieved not by pursuing wholeness merely on your own strength but by entering into God's plan for you as you walk in the footsteps of Jesus. It is believing that, yes, God is making all things new. He has destroyed sin and death; he is healing the division within you.

The kinds of reflections I have been making here I see mirrored in most books on spirituality written after Vatican II. None of them deny the essentials of spiritual conversion, such as repentance, detachment, prayer, penance, overcoming selfishness and living in charity. But the emphasis differs from pre-Vatican II spirituality.

Penance does not consist in punishing myself, or making prayer a time of self-analysis, or seeing the body as the great enemy in overcoming selfishness. Penance now is turning from self to God, letting go and letting Him work in my life, believing that He loves me and has saved me and is saving me each day. And the business of spirituality today is to get into contact with what God is doing in my life by lovingly embracing myself and others. Embracing is emphasized instead of renouncing, though renunciation is always involved in the selfless embrace.

Conversion, or the letting go of self, takes real penance, because I would prefer to be in complete charge of my own salvation. I want to control everything, including my thoughts and passions; I would rather control than surrender. To let God work and to take my attention off myself and focus on Him is to be converted to the Lord.

To be in God means overcoming what Dominican Father Matthew Fox calls our "fear of heaven." He once remarked that we are afraid of our own divinity. We are afraid of our having been made in the image and likeness of God the Creator. How true that is! How much faith is required to believe in my own goodness, to believe that good is more powerful than evil, and that all of us have been saved by Jesus Christ and that therefore we are worth loving. Life is worth living because I am worth loving; I can love others because God loves me.

The truth of this approach to God was brought home to me very dramatically a few years ago in Dijon, France. I was having supper in a small restaurant when I looked up and saw someone desperately trying to open the door. The waiter went over and opened it, and a young man in a wheelchair rolled in. He was crippled and deformed, and pushing him was a young woman in just about the same condition.

The waiter seated them at a table in the center of the restaurant, and they seemed totally oblivious to the embarrassment and stares of those around them. They were, in fact, beaming with joy.

Soon everyone in the restaurant was smiling and laughing. I called the waiter over and asked him what was happening, and he said simply, "They are on their honeymoon!" I am sure that is why everyone was so touched. They all realized that neither individual had ever thought he or she was lovable. But now each one can say, "Someone has come into my life and loves me, and I am beautiful, and I no longer notice others' stares, and I am no longer self-conscious and afraid." That is what God's love does for each of us, and that is what most spiritual writers are saying today.

There is in post-Vatican II thinking an increasingly positive regard for the world. The change here is clearly seen in the thinking of Thomas Merton as he moves from his earlier to later writings. There is a most striking change in Merton's view of the world from his first book, *The Seven Storey Mountain,* to a later book such as *Conjectures of a Guilty Bystander.*

The tone of *The Seven Storey Mountain* is that Merton is leaving a wicked world to enter a sort of new Eden at Gethsemani Abbey. The world "out there" is bad while the world "in spiritual solitude" is holy—a false split again. In *Conjectures of a Guilty Bystander* an older Thomas Merton recognizes his earlier unbalanced viewpoint—body and spirit are now merging. The older and wiser Merton writes:

> In Louisville, at the corner of Fourth and Walnut, in the center of the shopping district, I was suddenly overwhelmed with the realization that I loved all those people, that they were mine and I theirs, that we could not be alien to one another even though we were total strangers. It was like waking from a dream of separateness, of spurious self-isolation in a special world, the world of renunciation and supposed holiness. The whole illusion of a separate holy existence is a dream. . . .

> . . . though "out of the world" we are in the same world as everybody else, the world of the bomb, the world of race hatred, the world of technology, the world of mass media, big business, revolution, and all the rest. We take a different attitude to all these things, for we belong to God. Yet so

does everybody else belong to God. We just happen to be conscious of it, and to make a profession out of this consciousness. But does that entitle us to consider ourselves different, or even *better,* than others? The whole idea is preposterous.

Merton writes that he felt such relief at realizing the world was not an enemy that he "almost laughed out loud."

In conclusion, I would like to return to St. Francis. Before he received the stigmata, Francis was very hard on his own body. He starved it and subjected it to severe penances, and he drove himself to physical extremes of exhaustion. However, once he was touched by the Lord on Mount La Verna and received the stigmata, he began to ask his body's forgiveness for punishing it instead of embracing it as he had once embraced a leper.

And so it is with us. Once we finally touch the Lord and let him touch us, we are made whole. Then, as Francis writes in his last testament, "what before seemed repulsive is turned into sweetness of soul" for us because of that loving, holy touch of God. We move from an "I am a worthless worm" attitude to a "I am a beautiful and good person" attitude. And because of that new attitude of self-acceptance and self-love, instead of getting to heaven at last, our going there is itself a kind of heaven. And our lives, even in their continual conversion, become celebrations.

Surely we moderns are not losing our spirituality, as some contend. We are not giving up the pursuit of life in the Spirit. Rather, we are infusing the classical and tried elements of spiritual conversion and growth with a joy and celebration that stems from a renewed sense of our own worth because of the loving touch of God. And experiencing that loving touch of God in everything we touch and everything that touches us is what it means to live sacramentally, to have a sacramental vision of the world. That he embodied that vision is, I believe, the reason for the attraction of St. Francis of Assisi.

The Descent of Mount Subasio

I

It is beginning to cloud
over Mount Subasio and
two vague birds are flying
past my window and the
chickens in the yard above
are cackling their prophecy
before the silence of rain falls
and solitude begins.

II

I hear the wind
under the door
and the dog
barking in the yard
haunting
with childhood ghosts
this time and place
removed.

III

Always in Assisi
you are looking up,
climbing up, ascending.
Everything lifts, rises,
and your thighs ache
as your mind once did
on level ground.

IV

Here I am poet
under tiled roofs
above which the white moon

full of sun
hangs helpless at noon
gathering light
for its nocturnal climb
up the dark mountain.

V

This time Assisi is wind,
a strong wind, a cold wind
when the sun goes down.
And I remember
the year of the moon
and the year of rain
when the heart washed
down the streets
to the flooded fields
floating in poppies.
The air is dry now
and the sky is clear
except for high-riding
clouds at night when
you try to find the moon.

VI

Well, somehow,
out of all this,
the poem.
From these shards
the artifact emerges.
Whatever broke the life,
sending its pieces
over the desert floor,
brought together
the scattered heart
in this bowl
made whole again

in the search
for reasons.
And the evil
of its smashing
is its final
immortality.

VII

So the journey
to Assisi is over.
Now there is only
the desert from which
it sprang and fled
to the mountains,
this mountain, Subasio.
The desert is here
above the Umbrian plain.
The mountain was always
below the surface
of the mesa, and ascent
was descent into dream.

Letter to J.D.

Today is market day on our street. I look down from my third-floor window onto the blacktopped lot across the flurry of cars jockeying for a parking place, to the bar where you and your buddies were usually standing, looking up at the window where I write, comfortably insulated from your pain. One of them is in the hospital with jaundice and you died yesterday of internal bleeding. All three of you were alcoholics, as you told me so often standing at our door not pretending you wanted money for anything other than booze.

I was just finishing the final pages of this book when one of your friends rang the doorbell and told me you had died. He's scared because he knows he'll probably drink himself to death, too. He wants to break out of the vicious circle of despair inside and all around him. He remembers, as I do, how you would go away and dry out, one time for thirty days and then come back to this inner-city nightmare with no job, no hope of a job, the same buddies saying maybe one drink will help.

You were thirty-four years old, and the last time I talked to you, you were angry because we made you wait downstairs while we went to the money drawer to help you out, and you said black guys weren't good enough to come in. So we let you in and you cleverly laid guilt on us for a half hour and said that marvelous meal prayer and told us how you were finally breaking out, going to nursing school, finally going to be free. What happened, and how could I sit up here writing, watching you guys die, doing nothing? And what difference will a book like this make to you and my other friends at the bar?

They call our street Pleasant Street, but it was anything but pleasant for you, though you made it so for me as I talked with you and gave you money and felt superior. Money always does that, and so as you leave us, I'd like to tell you about a saint you could understand and who understood you and knew how you were feeling when we insensitively left you in the hall instead of inviting you into our home.

His name was St. Francis and he wasn't an alcoholic, but he knew what it meant to be addicted. He saw his father addicted to money, and he saw himself getting that way, too. So he gave it all away (can you imagine that?) and started begging in the streets and living like you on the outside of the houses you beg from. He wouldn't have given you *some* money; he would have given you *all* his money and then gone out in the street with you and pushed you till you shaped up and went to a program; and then he would have seen to it that you had something to come back to when you were finally dried out.

St. Francis lived eight hundred years ago, but he was plenty streetwise. You couldn't have conned him, and he was tough enough to stick by you till you did what you had to do to save yourself. I'm sure he was more where you were than where I am, and he would have had about as much use for my fancy words as you did. He didn't talk much; he *did* things for people, and he wouldn't go only halfway, or less, as I did with you.

You would have recognized right off that he was a preacher, a man of the Lord, and I'm sure you'll know him when you meet him up there. Chances are, he'll be one of the first to come and put his arms around you. When he asks about me, don't tell him I had money to give you instead of love, or if you do, tell him we're trying and not to give up on us. You see, we haven't learned to overcome shame, as you had to do every time you rang the doorbell. We, or at least I, am still trying to be respectable and do what Catholic priests are supposed to do, the way they're supposed to do it. I'm still hesitating to live the Gospel fully because it's so scandalous and would make a lot of people angry, and I don't have the courage Francis had to ignore the self-righteous and listen to the Lord instead.

And don't tell St. Francis that I was writing another book about him when you died. He wouldn't like that. He would wonder why I wasn't writing a book about you and your friends, or why I had time to write books at all when Jesus was out there on the streets suffering from alcoholism and was hungry and cold and in despair.

St. Francis had street eyes, and he knew where God really lived, and he couldn't understand why other people were looking for him in all the wrong places. To St. Francis, God is a beggar, and he often hangs out in front of a bar. Don't tell him that I keep passing him by on the way to and from my desk. Or if you do, tell him I used to talk with you sometimes, OK?

> Murray Bodo
> Pleasant Street
> Cincinnati

SOURCES

NOTE: Unless otherwise indicated, all quotations from *St. Francis of Assisi: Writing and Early Biographies: English Omnibus of the Sources for the Life of St. Francis* (hereafter referred to as OS), ed. Marion Habig (Chicago: Franciscan Herald Press, 1973), are the author's own reworking of existing translations.

INTRODUCTION

"Francis, go and repair . . ." *Legend of the Three Companions,* chap. V, no. 13.
"Listen to me . . ." Ibid., chap. VI, no. 20.
"The Lord gave me . . ." *Testament of St. Francis.*
"O Lord, I beg . . ." *Little Flowers of St. Francis,* Third Consideration on the Stigmata.
"I have done . . ." Thomas of Celano, *Second Life of St. Francis,* chap. CLXII, no. 214.

POVERTY

"Holy Poverty stands . . ." *Sacrum Commercium,* Prologue, no. 1.
"The Son of God . . ." Ibid., Prologue, no. 2.
"The other virtues . . ." Ibid.
"One day . . ." *Legend of the Three Companions,* chap. IV, no. 11.
"As he is riding . . ." Ibid.

MAKING PEACE

"Francis picked up . . ." Adolf Holl, *The Last Christian* (Garden City, N.Y.: Doubleday and Company, 1980), p. 171.

LIVING THE GOSPEL

"We should not have . . ."   *Rule of 1221*, chap. 8.

REPAIRING GOD'S HOUSE

"Most High . . ."   Francis' *Prayer Before the Crucifix*.
"A tender and compassionate . . ."   *Legend of the Three Companions*, chap. V, nos. 13, 14.
"From now on . . ."   Ibid., chap. VII, no. 21.

LEARNING TO PRAY

"His father goes round . . ."   *Legend of the Three Companions*, chap. VI, nos. 16, 17.
"On the steps . . ."   Ibid., chap. III, no. 10.
"He is looking . . ."   *Little Flowers of St. Francis*, Second Consideration on the Stigmata.
"Make all of your time . . ."   Thomas of Celano, *Second Life of St. Francis*, chaps. LXI, LXII, LXIII.

PRAYER AND ACTION

"The focus of this story from . . ."   *Little Flowers of St. Francis*, chap. 16.

THE MIRROR OF ST. CLARE

All quotations from St. Clare are a reworking of the translations in *Francis and Clare: The Complete Works*, trans. and Introduction by Regis J. Armstrong, O.F.M., Cap., and Ignatius Brady, O.F.M. (New York: Paulist Press; Toronto: Ramsey, 1982).

"The Lord Promises . . ."   *First Letter of St. Clare to Blessed Agnes of Prague*, no. 25.
"What a praiseworthy . . ."   Ibid., no. 30.
"Since the great and good Lord . . ."   Ibid., no. 19.
"For the Lord himself . . ."   *Testament of St. Clare*, no. 6.
"Because the vision . . ."   *Fourth Letter of St. Clare to Blessed Agnes of Prague*, nos. 14–19.
"Look at the edges . . ."   Ibid., nos. 19–26.

NOTE: For a further development of the mirror imagery of the Middle Ages, cf. Frederick Goldin, *The Mirror of Narcissus in the Courtly Love Lyric*. (Ithaca, N.Y.: Cornell University Press, 1967).

THE CAVE

NOTE: For a further development of the ideas contained in paragraph 4, cf. Eloi Leclerc, *The Canticle of Creatures: Symbols of Union.* (Chicago: Franciscan Herald Press, 1970), pp. 137–47.

OBEDIENCE

"He is sitting . . ." Thomas of Celano, *Second Life of St. Francis,* chap. CXII.
"But Francis thought . . ." Ibid.

FATHER AND SON

"When Pietro . . ." *Legend of the Three Companions,* chap. VII, no. 23.
"When he heard . . ." Ibid.
"Meanwhile he kept working . . ." Ibid., no. 24.

A CEREMONY OF INVESTITURE

"There is a contract . . ." Thomas of Celano, *Second Life of St. Francis,* chap. XL, no. 70.
"It is absolutely forbidden . . ." *Rule of 1223,* chap. 2.

INTIMACY

"Gathering handfuls of snow . . ." Thomas of Celano, *Second Life of St. Francis,* chap. LXXXII, no. 117.
"It does not know how . . ." Ibid., chap. XCVII, no. 134.
"If he who lent me . . ." Ibid., chap. XCVI, no. 133.
"Tendencies which inform . . ." Philip Novak, *New Catholic World,* vol. 225, no. 1348 (July/August 1982), p. 194.
"Love, love, my heart . . ." George T. Peck, *The Fool of God: Jacopone da Todi* (University, Ala.: University of Alabama Press, 1980), p. 182.
"I find you . . ." *The Selected Poetry of Rainer Maria Rilke,* ed. and trans. Stephen Mitchell (New York: Random House, 1982), p. 5.
"I was once . . ." *Sacrum Commercium,* chap. III, no. 25.
"From then on . . ." Ibid., no. 30.
"Thus it was . . ." Ibid., chap. II, no. 19.
"Before the Most High . . ." Ibid., chap. III, no. 31.
"My God and my all." *Little Flowers of St. Francis,* chap. 2.

"Oh, how glorious . . ." *Francis and Clare: The Complete Works.* (New York: Paulist Press, 1982), p. 63.

THE EXCHANGE OF LOVE

"When God gave me . . ." *Testament of St. Francis.*
"Always searching . . ." *Admonitions of St. Francis,* Admonition XVI.
"I strictly forbid . . ." *Testament of St. Francis.*
"Those who embraced . . ." Ibid.
"With us . . ." Thomas Merton, *The Wisdom of the Desert* (New York: New Directions, 1960), pp. 9–10.
"Once when Francis . . ." Thomas of Celano, *First Life of St. Francis,* chap. VII, no. 107.

NOTE: For a further treatment of *amour voulu,* cf. Rosemary Haughton, *The Passionate God* (New York: Paulist Press, 1981), pp. 58–63.

"Not long after . . ." *Legend of the Three Companions,* chap. III, no. 7.
"The bride was . . ." Ibid.

EVIL

"In every work . . ." Thomas of Celano, *Second Life of St. Francis,* chap. CXXIV, no. 165.
"Francis, what you have . . ." Ibid., chap. V, no. 9.
"Father, I ask you . . ." *Little Flowers of St. Francis,* chap. 8.
"The story of the Damietta Prostitute . . ." Ibid., chap. 24.

JOURNEY TO ROME

"Obedience and reverence to his holiness . . ." *Rule of 1223,* chap. 1.

THE WOMAN OF THE DESERT

"My son, go . . ." *Legend of the Three Companions,* chap. XII, no. 50.
"In a desert . . ." Ibid.
"I am that poor woman . . ." Ibid., no. 51.
"He seemed to be walking . . ." Ibid., no. 53.

"The irresistible . . ." Leclerc, op. cit., pp. 150–51.
"I'd like to go . . ." Robert Frost, *Complete Poems* (New York: Henry Holt & Company, 1949), p. 153.
"The heights of the spirit . . ." Leclerc, op. cit., p. 151.

FRANCISCAN LIFE TODAY

"We are ourselves . . ." *The Divine Office. The Liturgy of the Hours,* vol. III (London, Sydney, Dublin: Collins, Dwyer, Talbot, 1974), p. 91.
"We should not want . . ." *Letter to the Faithful.*

THE WAY OF DIALOGUE

"When they go . . ." *Rule of 1223,* chap. 3.
"No matter where . . ." *Rule of 1221,* chap. 7.

THE WAY OF COMMUNION

"Should speak only . . ." *Rule of 1223,* chap. 9.
"I would like you . . ." *Letter to a Minister.*

THE WAY OF MORTIFICATION

"One story in . . ." Thomas of Celano, *Second Life of St. Francis,* chap. XV, no. 22; *Legend of Perugia,* no. 1; *Mirror of Perfection,* chap. 27; St. Bonaventure, *Major Legend,* chap. 5, no. 7.

THE WAY OF FREEDOM

"Each mortal . . ." *Poems of Gerard Manley Hopkins,* ed. W. H. Gardner and N. H. Mackenzie (New York, London: Oxford University Press, 1948), p. 95.
"And be one . . ." Frost, op. cit., p. 131.
"I have done . . ." Thomas of Celano, *Second Life of St. Francis,* chap. CLXII, no. 214.
"The just man . . ." *Poems of Gerard Manley Hopkins,* p. 95.

JESUS

"O Lord, I beg . . ." *Little Flowers of St Francis,* Third Consideration on the Stigmata.

180   SOURCES

THE CANTICLE OF BROTHER SUN

"Most High, All-Powerful . . ."   OS, pp. 130–31.
"Deep down things . . ."   *Poems of Gerard Manley Hopkins*, p. 70.
"The Rule and life . . ."   *Rule of 1221*, chap. 1.
"The day is coming . . ."   *Legend of the Three Companions*, chap. II, no. 4.
"He urged even . . ."   Thomas of Celano, *Second Life of St. Francis*, chap. CLXIII, no. 217.
"We ought to . . ."   Admonition VI.
"Be ahead . . ."   *The Selected Poetry of Rainer Maria Rilke*, p. 245.

THE JOURNEY INWARD

"Who could feel . . ."   "The Wisdom of the Heart," from *The Henry Miller Reader*. (New York: New Directions, 1959), pp. 258–59.
"We read the Book . . ."   *New York Times*, October 26, 1982, p. 14.
"The transubstantiation of matter . . ."   Nikos Kazantzakis, *St. Francis* (New York: Simon and Schuster, 1962), p. 12.
"All praise be yours . . ."   OS, p. 130.

AFTERWORD

"In Louisville . . ."   Thomas Merton, *Conjectures of a Guilty Bystander* (Garden City, N.Y.: Doubleday and Company, 1968), pp. 156–57.
"What before . . ."   *Testament of St. Francis*.